NOW WHAT?!

CONVERSATIONS
about
COLLEGE,
GRADUATION,
and the
NEXT STEP

ARI KING

Now What?! Conversations about College, Graduation, and the Next Step
Ari King

Published by Ari King

Editor: Grace Duggan
Designer: Kelly Baker

ISBN: 978-0-9887530-0-6

Printed in the USA

For Nancy Alberti and
Emma Blumstein

Acknowledgements

First and foremost, I would like to thank Beth Tondreau for all her help and guidance. I couldn't have done this without her. I am, and forever will be, grateful.

To everyone who contributed to the Kickstarter™ campaign: thank you. It was a truly humbling experience to see so many people have an interest in and support for this book. Thank you.

To my brother, Monroe King: I will never accomplish as much as you have. Although you might not have known it, you were an inspiration every time I sat down to write.

To my mom, Roberta Aron: I could write a separate book about what makes you so special and how much I love you. But for now, I want you to know that I am one hundred percent certain that you are the greatest mother in the history of the world. I love you.

Kickstarter Donors

Thank you to everyone who contributed to this project, including

Lindsay Abrams, Aline, Susan Ansley, Jeff Aron, Roberta Aron, Jared Ashe, Jake Bauch, Alison Brower, Zachary Butlein, Steve Buyske, Tyler Byrne, Paul Chapman, Ernest Chen, Ann and Glenn Cohen, Sean Collins, JoAnn Copperund, Rachel Cushing, Ann Daniels, Alicia Dantzker, William Doyel, John Edwards, Maren Ellingboe, Randy and Lynn Ellingboe, David Enelow, Benjamin Falik, Bill Falik, Brittany Fowler, Allie Freed, Donald Freed, Julia Freedman, Rebecca Friedman, Shana Garrity, Ken Gibson and Diane Murphy, Gabriel González-Kreisberg, Neil Gordon, Sarice Greenstein, Claire Griffin, Janienne Hackett, Justin Haden, Keiko Hamano, Jordan Harris, Jana Heaton, Tristan Helms, Will Houghteling, Tyler Infelise, Elizabeth Isono, Rebecca Johnson, Noa Kaplan, Rebecca Karasik, Steve and Lynn Katz, Michelle Katz, David Kohan, Chi Le, Netta Levran, Rita Denise Lewis, Miranda Limonczenko, Tyler Lohman, Kym Lugman, Adrian Ma, Rebecca Maloney, John D. Menke, Conrad Murphy, Joy Nelson, Bruce Nye, Risa Nye, Holly Ovington, Max Owen-Dunow, Julie Palley, Matt Palley, Pasternak, Anthony Phalen, Otis Poisson, Leslie Powell, Pamela Quezada, Lauren Racah, Rebecca, David Wen Riccardi-Zhu, Lisa Ross, Sarah, Jon Sargent, Seek Films, Jim Shepherd, Yuki Shiraji, Derek Silverman, Marlon Simpkins, Jesse Spear, Kirk London Staley, Lauren Statman, Aaron Stein, Thorild Urdal, Scott Verges, Alan Wells, Josh Wessler, Alexis Wilkes, Lori M. Winters, Josh Wood, Krista Marie Yu, and Jonathan Zingman.

Contents

Introduction

Upon graduating, you have presumably spent four years in an environment where there is a strong emphasis on getting into college and graduating, but not usually a blueprint for when you get out. Okay, now what?! It's a simple phrase that can be applied to almost any situation and all graduates. In college, once you receive your diploma, you are at the end of one journey, but also at the beginning of another. In high school, you were encouraged to play sports, do community service, run for student council, play an instrument, and take the SATs, all to look better for colleges. College acts as a giant umbrella when you transition from high school. There are majors to declare, dorms to live in, and peers to bond with. Not only can you can rely on older students, family members, and the college's staff to assist you, guide you, and answer questions, but all of the options are presented to you. However, when you graduate from college, there is little to no structure about what comes next. So what are you supposed to do?

Before I even collected my paycheck from the first job I had out of college, I started a blog to document my post-graduation struggles. It wasn't funny at the time, but I convinced myself that one day, I would look back on my situation—ramen noodles, sleeping on couches, the overall thought of, "Why the hell am I in New York City?!"—and laugh. A few entries piqued my interest as to what my friends and peers were up to. I would send e-mails or call friends to check in, see how their job interviews went, or just shoot the shit. I soon realized that I wasn't the only one who was unsure and wondering what would come next, especially since I, along with most of my friends, had graduated in the spring of 2009, one of the worst times to graduate in decades.

After spending that first summer at home in California, I moved to New York. I didn't have a job or an apartment, and even though the economy was bad, New York seemed to provide the best opportunity for a college graduate. It offered different industries as well as high turnover in hospitality positions in restaurants, bars, and hotels. I stayed with a friend who was a senior at New York University at the time, along with his five roommates. My days consisted of waking up extremely early not because my alarm went off, but because of the smell of stale beer in the air, August humidity, and overall discomfort from sleeping on a couch that had been handed down from college student to college student. I would go onto Craigslist knowing a migraine was not too far away and look for jobs under every category from "Government" and "Education" to "Russian-speaking Nanny" and "Security Guard."

I came up with the idea for this book after thinking about how there are guidebooks to cities that would list where to eat and what to do, and that there should be something comparable for those who are finishing college. College graduation is, to some extent, similar to going somewhere you have never been before, except it isn't a vacation or business trip. I wanted to get as many stories and as much advice as possible; I was just as eager to hear what it was like to get a job with a big company like Google or Goldman Sachs as I was for the person living at home, working as a babysitter, and trying to build their photography portfolio. About four months into my endeavor, I wanted to go a little bit further and thought it might be interesting to get the stories of older, more established graduates, so they, too, could recount their senior year and what they did during their "first year out."

I sought out as many different industries and professions as I could in order to better relate to college graduates and people in general. While most books for those out of college tend to focus on tips and strategies for landing the perfect job, or how to network properly and correctly tailor your résumé, few, if any, books are centered on the feelings, thoughts, and sense of unknown that recent graduates experience. If you are a biology major who wants to go to medical school, or a music major who is now interested in becoming a writer, you will be able to find multiple stories that are informational, inspiring, and full of practical advice. A significant number of graduates featured in this book started off with a job unrelated to what they studied in college, let alone one they had an interest in. Others were doing exactly what they planned for while they were in college, while some were taking a circuitous path as they navigated their post-college lives; the chapters in this book reflect such a variety of paths. The first part of each story or interview gives some back story on the individual: their thoughts and feelings during senior year, what ideas they had for after graduation and how and why they changed, and the steps they took while planning their first year out. The latter half consists of points that the reader can take away from each story: senior year regrets, what they learned through college, thoughts on living in the real world, and advice for graduates.

Everyone has a story to tell about their senior year in college and the first year out. For some, it was a struggle capped with anxiety, doubt, questions, and feelings of failure. For others, it was a year spent traveling, preparing for graduate school, working a random job, and dealing with the unknown as to what would come next. No matter what your story is, and whether or not you think it is interesting, you still have one.

The
Know-It-Alls

THOSE WHO HAVE ALWAYS KNOWN
WHAT THEY WANTED TO DO AND
TOOK SUCCESSFUL STEPS TO DO IT.

Thomas Kail

WHAT I STUDIED	WHAT I DO
AMERICAN HISTORY	THEATER DIRECTOR (*Magic/Bird*, *Lombardi*, *In the Heights*)

CLASS OF 1999

"I really liked being in school for eight semesters. It was the perfect amount of time. When graduation came, I was ready to go."

During his senior year, Thomas decided that he would give himself a full year after graduation to find work in theater, even though he had studied for and taken the LSAT. "I took the LSAT because I thought, 'Why not? I'm already in school mode. Gonna be a whole lot easier to study and take it now than later down the road.'" Although he was a history major, he developed a love for theater, music, and entertainment, which led to the co-creation of a freestyle hip-hop dance group while in college. He wanted to explore working in theater, so he applied for only one job during his senior year as an administrative assistant in the literary office of the Arena Stage in Washington, D.C.

"It was a lovely interview," Thomas said. "About two weeks later, I get a handwritten note. Very graciously written. It said, 'I really like you and think you would be great for this position. There are twenty-five other candidates who all have M.F.A. [degrees]. If I hired you, I would lose my job.' So I graduated without a job. I was never concerned with the idea that I might never find a job. I felt like I did things in college to the best of my abilities, and I was good with that."

With no backup plan, Thomas reached out to a college friend's father who had a friend that worked for a small theater in New Jersey. "I never wanted to go to the New York area. I didn't want to be a small fish in a big pond. I was more interested in blazing my own trail, but since D.C. didn't work out, I had to." An interview was set up for the New Jersey theater, but before it took place, Thomas decided to make some changes to his résumé. "At the bottom of my CV, I wrote, 'P.S. I make a mean cup of coffee.'" When he walked into the interview, he noticed that the only part of his résumé that had any notes was the part about the coffee. "During the interview I was asked if I really could make a cup of coffee, and if I knew how to drive a fifteen-passenger van. I said yes to both, but only the coffee part was true."

Thomas began as the driver for all of the actors, working his way up to assistant director after he took it upon himself to take notes during rehearsals, which led to his promotion. One night, as he was dropping the actors off at their apartments, he called the director and asked if he could stop by. "I told him I had some notes on the show, and next thing I know, he has a notepad with him and a drink. I stayed there until 2:00 a.m. going over what I had to say about the show." Shortly thereafter, Thomas, twenty-three at the time, was promoted to associate artistic director. As he began to learn more and more about theater and directing, he continued to work with Freestyle Love Supreme, the improv group he and some college friends had created as undergrads. Members of the group, including Thomas, went on to write, act, direct, and compose for *In the Heights*.

Senior Year Regrets:

"I found that during my senior year I was able to really focus. I did everything to the best of my abilities, so I don't have any regrets. I was best at throwing everything at one thing as opposed to being half-hearted with several things. I like having one thing to go after."

What College Taught Me:

"Surround yourself with people who know things you don't."

Life in the Real World:

"I was ready to work hard, so that was not a shock. I wanted to roll up my sleeves and start. Once you get out of the world of academia you have colleagues who are twenty-five years older than you. You are twenty-two, they are sixty. I learned whom I could ask questions from and what it is like to interact with people from different generations."

Advice for Graduates:

"Put yourself in as many positions as you can stand to meet people that are different than you already know. I worked [at the theater] job that had eight full-time employees. I drove the van. I swept the stage. I wrote the program. They needed a walk-on role; it was me because they didn't have to pay me, so I stood in.

"Whatever you are doing try to do, do it as well as it can be done. Don't think it's below you or below your education level."

MY FIRST APARTMENT

"My first apartment after college was in Hoboken, New Jersey. It was a basement in an apartment owned by an old Italian lady. I had to enter through the garage door. No windows. There were mirrors everywhere, and red velour on the floor. All I ate for eighteen months was Campbell's Chunky Soup, tomato soup, and tuna fish. There was no kitchen. Then I moved into a former dentist's office. [It] had windows, and [that] was a huge selling point."

Peter Blauner

WHAT I STUDIED

ENGLISH AND
GOVERNMENT STUDIES

CLASS OF 1982

WHAT I DO

AWARD-WINNING AUTHOR
OF SIX NOVELS,
INCLUDING
Slow Motion Riot

"I was in a dreamlike fog of confusion and cloudy aspiration."

By the time he graduated, Peter was experiencing "itchy, bristling impatience." As that impatience manifested, he began looking forward to completing his education and starting his career as a writer. "I was very focused on getting out of college and into the real world. I wanted to be a writer and I wanted to engage in experiences that I could use as source material for fiction," he said. Although Peter was happy to begin a life after college, he did have second thoughts about his situation; he wished he were a little more prepared. "I wanted to get out and get my hands dirty. It was only after I got out that I realized I could have used a little more time in the washroom."

As a result of his successful internship the summer after graduation through the Magazine Publishers of America (now the Association of Magazine Media), Peter was promoted to fact-checker with *New York* magazine. "I'd built up a portfolio of my writing, which proved to be largely irrelevant because good college writing doesn't impress that many people in professional fields. You're going to pay your dues anyway, so there are no shortcuts, and by the time you graduate, your writing should be developing to a new level anyway. Nevertheless, I'd say it was important for me personally to have done the preparation, so that I knew I had the desire and discipline to try to make a living this way."

Senior Year Regrets:

"Instead of going straight to New York, it probably would have been wiser to have pursued a newspaper job in a small town. I would've gotten more hands-on experience and possibly learned more about a place that's easier to define and comprehend than New York City. I would have started looking for an apartment in New York at least six months before I graduated, because I knew that's where I wanted to be."

What College Taught Me:

"The value of lasting friendships and some small measure of self-sufficiency."

Life in the Real World:

"I think it's important to subscribe to the old-school virtues of being ready, willing, and able."

Advice for Graduates:

"Older adults often tell recent graduates to just be yourself when you go on your first job interviews. I actually think that's a mistake. How do you know who you are when you're twenty-two? What makes you think your potential employer cares who you are? That's not as simple as it sounds. Now that I'm grizzled and old (or older), I recognize that the young person who's ready to walk through a door when it's open has a great advantage over the person who hesitates, vacillates, or thinks they're too good to have to respond promptly. I would've rolled my eyes if I heard this advice at twenty-two (actually, I'm sure I did), but sometimes you really do only get one chance to have a different kind of life. And if you don't take that opportunity, maybe there's somebody who literally walked across the desert to get here who will. And the people who are in a position to give you that break want to recognize some eager, hard-working version of themselves in you. But they don't want to work that hard to see it. With someone else primed in the waiting room, can you blame them?"

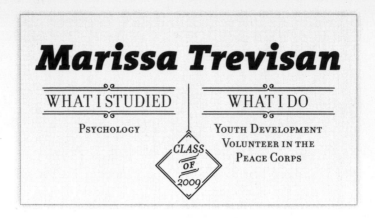

Marissa Trevisan

WHAT I STUDIED | WHAT I DO

PSYCHOLOGY | YOUTH DEVELOPMENT VOLUNTEER IN THE PEACE CORPS

CLASS OF 2009

"Despite having no indoor plumbing, bathing with a bucket, and going to the bathroom in a latrine, it's a pretty sweet life."

With little on Marissa's mind during her freshman year besides running around and screaming, "College!" she took three and a half years to figure out what she wanted to do after graduation: join the Peace Corps. In her senior year she applied to the Peace Corps, AmeriCorps, a fellowship at a charter school, and teaching and tutoring positions. Fortunately, she was accepted at her first choice, the Peace Corps, and is, as of this writing, a Youth Development Volunteer in El Salvador.

During winter break of her senior year, Marissa applied to several positions she found on Idealist. "I applied to the Peace Corps and several other jobs, mostly teaching and tutoring positions at charter schools in the Boston area. My hope was to have a job before graduation, and after all those job applications, there was a lot of follow-up and waiting." As the waiting game stretched from weeks to months, Marissa became convinced that after all her interviews, she was going to graduate without a job. However, two days before graduation, she was accepted into the Peace Corps in

El Salvador. Even though she was extremely proud of herself and excited to have something lined up, she found the idea of being so far away from her family and friends daunting.

"I was definitely sad that school was ending, because I knew I would be so far from my family and friends, but at the same time, I was pretty excited about the Peace Corps," she said. "While I was ready to leave college, I would have been happy finding more local employment and spending some time with family and friends in the Brookline/Boston area."

Senior Year Regrets:

"After a while, I stopped applying for jobs because I had my heart set on Peace Corps. If I hadn't been accepted, I would have been in a tough spot because I had already turned down my one other job offer at a charter school in the hopes of joining the Peace Corps. Luckily it worked out, but I probably should have continued looking for other jobs in the meantime."

What College Taught Me:

"Traveling abroad during [my] junior year in Madrid, Spain, helped me to expand my cultural perspective, and I'm thankful for that because it's part of the reason I'm in El Salvador today."

Life in the Real World:

"The 'real world' in El Salvador was a real shock for me. The first two months in my community were probably the toughest two months of my life, emotionally speaking. I thought about going home almost every single day. I felt isolated, alone, and desperate. Now, more than a year later, I have adapted, integrated into my community, and made a home for myself here. The first few months in my site, I ate beans and tortillas for breakfast, lunch, and dinner. Now I've worked some variation into my diet, but I still eat beans and tortillas every day."

Advice for Graduates:

"Apply to *a lot* of jobs. Also, do your best to read credible books while you're going on interviews. On one interview, the interviewer asked me what I was currently reading for pleasure. I told him *Harry Potter*. Not the best answer."

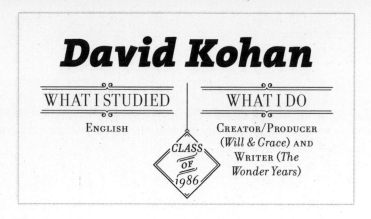

David Kohan

WHAT I STUDIED

ENGLISH

CLASS OF 1986

WHAT I DO

CREATOR/PRODUCER
(*Will & Grace*) AND
WRITER (*The
Wonder Years*)

"If you go into college thinking about the job you are going to have when you graduate, you are missing the whole point."

Like many undergraduates, David had a vague notion of going to law school. That interest all but disappeared by the time he was a senior, when his chief concern was, "Am I going to find the thing I'm going to hook into, and am I going to be homeless?" He was sad that school was coming to a close, but happy to know that the last four years had helped shape him in ways he never thought possible. "I had the sense that college was a kind of a hammock in my life," he said. "I was comfortable and totally independent, but at the same time protected. [I] didn't have to take financial responsibility yet."

David believed college was the best time to try several different approaches and (re)invent oneself, so he wanted to see what classes he became interested in and make a career decision from there. As an English major, he was enamored with writing, but also had a knack for entertainment. "I got really interested in stuff I was studying. If you get excited about learning a certain thing, you are so far ahead. Don't take a required class just to take it."

After graduating, David moved in with his parents and then with his girlfriend in Los Angeles, where he landed a job as an apprentice writer on *It's Gary Shandling's Show*. "I was so convinced I didn't belong there that I maybe said fifteen words over that eight-week span. I really thought that I maybe should have gone to law school, but everything good that ever happened to me was because I was willing to take a risk, and that risk was to stick in entertainment."

Following David's apprenticeship, a colleague put him in touch with the late director Sydney Pollack, who soon hired him as an assistant. It was the opportunity he was looking for to see how the business worked from the inside out.

Senior Year Regrets:

"In terms of attitude of life, I would have been more open to taking risks. By the time you are thirty, you should [have taken] two or three risks. At twenty-three you think you have a lot to lose, but you don't."

What College Taught Me:

"I learned how to love and appreciate ideas."

Life in the Real World:

"The scariest thing is the anticipation. Once you are doing it, it becomes your new reality. When you have some job and you are paying the rent and you work feverishly at night, that is your real world. It's not so depressing when you are doing it. The thinking about it in some kind of grand terms like, 'Is this the rest of my life?' is no good. If you think your goal is being partner in a law firm, then it's like being in a pie-eating contest and winning and the reward is a lifetime supply of pie. Believe in yourself and follow through."

Advice for Graduates:

"Don't assume that people in charge know more than you. They don't, necessarily. Don't be cowed by the experience of those in charge. If your ideas are good, and in your heart you know [if] they are good or not, then you need to follow through. Say to yourself, 'This is what I want and this is what I'm going for.'"

Dana Gal

WHAT I STUDIED

NEUROSCIENCE AND
BEHAVIOR

CLASS OF 2009

WHAT I DO

CLINICAL STUDY
COORDINATOR AT
CHILDREN'S
HOSPITAL BOSTON

"I was one hundred percent in party mode."

Both after graduating high school and college, Dana had one thing she wanted to be in life: a doctor. As a result, she placed a high level of importance on finding a job that would strengthen her medical school applications. "Med schools look for very sequential applications, and applicants can do a variety of different things in their lives, but, ultimately, the schools want to see how those activities and jobs have prepared them to be doctors. In my senior year, I basically applied to every job I could find that would help me." At the same time, she still took advantage of being a senior in college and went out four times a week.

Having such a great college experience made it that much harder for Dana to move on and get ready to graduate. She applied to as many jobs as she could during her senior year, but was coming up empty. After three interviews for three different positions and tirelessly checking the job boards for multiple hospitals, she was beginning to feel less optimistic.

"One Saturday night, I went to see some friends and I brought over a handle of Jack Daniel's. I met one of my friend's roommates.

She first explained to me how much she liked whiskey, and then said that both her parents were in clinical research and she'd see if they had any ideas." The next day, Dana had an e-mail from the girl's mother; a colleague needed a research assistant. A day later, following a successful interview, she had a job.

Senior Year Regrets:

"I don't know if I would change any of it. It worked out pretty well. The only thing that was not awesome was that I had to start work one week after graduation, so I barely got a break, but it was such a tough economy that negotiating the details wasn't really an option."

What College Taught Me:

"Always bring Jack Daniel's to a pre-game party, because you never know what your friend's roommate's parents do. No one is going to want to hire someone without social skills and interesting life experiences."

Life in the Real World:

"Speak up. The more you ask for help, the more likely you are to get it. That being said, know when to shut up. People like to help other people, but no one likes whiners."

Advice for Graduates:

"Persistence is the only reason I got a job. Make the most of senior week, relax as much as possible, plan a cool spring break trip. Get out of the library sometimes. You have the rest of your life to apply to jobs, but only a couple years in college, and I think it is incredibly important to make those lasting friendships and connections that will support you through the rest. My advice to anyone searching for jobs would be to take advantage of any connections you can find, even if you've just met the person that night, and don't necessarily settle for a job you don't want. Delay the acceptance date as much as possible if you're unsure, because something might come up."

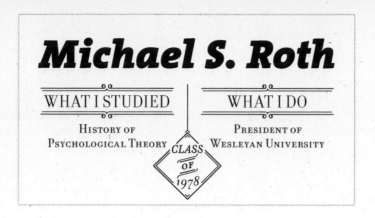

Michael S. Roth

WHAT I STUDIED
HISTORY OF PSYCHOLOGICAL THEORY

WHAT I DO
PRESIDENT OF WESLEYAN UNIVERSITY

CLASS OF 1978

"It is so important for everyone to develop networks of relationships."

Michael believed he wanted to be one of three things as he began his college career: a writer, psychologist, or lawyer. For him, college was a transformative experience, as his professors introduced him to new ways of learning, which, in turn, opened his eyes to new possibilities. While in college, he developed an interest in academia, with his chief concern becoming whether he should further his education immediately after graduating or get some work experience first. Keeping all of his options open, he applied to various psychology-related jobs and graduate schools. "I was very focused on a senior thesis for a good part of the year. I was also president of Alpha Delta Phi (a co-ed fraternity), had a serious girlfriend, and wasn't at all eager to be leaving college."

In March of his senior year, Michael received a job offer for a research position at a psychiatric hospital as well as a fellowship for a graduate school program. Excited by the opportunities that both situations offered him, but knowing he could choose only one, he pursued the fellowship and enrolled in a Ph.D.

program two months after graduating and squatting on various campuses with friends.

"While in grad school, I interviewed as I was finishing up. I looked into the backgrounds of the people in my field at the relevant schools. I didn't know what I was doing, but I got lucky and got a job as a professor at Scripps College."

Q&A

Senior Year Regrets:
"Nothing."

What College Taught Me:
"I found out what I loved to do, learned how to find ways to get better at it, and learned how to live well with very different kinds of people. I made great friends who expanded my sense of what life could offer. I learned to work very hard and to find that work enormously gratifying."

Life in the Real World:
"I'm still at college (as the president). It is real to me!"

Advice for Graduates:
"Don't worry about how many times you are turned down. You only need one job."

TWO INTERVIEWS

"Once I was interviewed by a group of patients at a psychiatric hospital who asked me if I thought they were crazy. I said yes and I got the job offer. I was interviewed for a prestigious fellowship and they asked me about a transformative negative experience. I told them about a fight I'd gotten into, and I could tell they were appalled by the physical violence. But it was too late. I didn't get the fellowship."

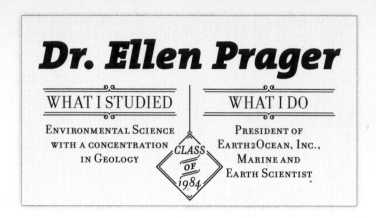

Dr. Ellen Prager

WHAT I STUDIED

ENVIRONMENTAL SCIENCE WITH A CONCENTRATION IN GEOLOGY

CLASS OF 1984

WHAT I DO

PRESIDENT OF EARTH2OCEAN, INC., MARINE AND EARTH SCIENTIST

"Recent graduates should not expect to start at the top; low-level, low-paying jobs set the stage for entry into many fields and allow you to make the contacts and build the experience needed to progress to higher levels."

Ellen had no idea what she wanted to do as a freshman. "I spent a semester away from [college] in my junior year studying tropical marine science at the West Indies Laboratory in Saint Croix, and that had a huge impact on my career and life," she said. The experience was so positive that she stayed through the summer in Saint Croix after her program ended and worked for an underwater laboratory, learning about science and diving while getting hands-on experience. As a result, she returned to the United States energized and ready for senior year and life after college. "I was thrilled to be back, playing sports, studying, and spending time with friends, but, at the same time, I was extremely excited about marine science and doing more in the field."

She returned to the West Indies once she graduated, working as a laboratory and diving assistant for a few years before going to graduate school. "Those few years were instrumental in my career, partly because I had wonderful mentors at both college and the lab in Saint Croix. I was extremely well prepared for graduate school by both experiences, and took away an independent, hard-working ethic."

Senior Year Regrets:

"Nothing, really. I sent out a lot of résumés, but was extremely fortunate to be offered exactly the job I wanted. Persistence and hard work paid off for me."

What College Taught Me:

"It is very important to build on the skills and contacts your college enables, and to proactively go after opportunities; for the most part, they won't come to you."

Life in the Real World:

"The real world is what you make of it! There will be good as well as bad, and no job is perfect. One of the things you need to do is to discover what you don't want to do, along with what you do. All of your experiences will help you to find your real passion."

Advice for Graduates:

"Do not be afraid to ask for help, contacts, or advice from people in your field and professors. Persistence and hard work pay off. Do your homework for job interviews, show your passion and willingness to work hard, and always be professional. For jobs, be prepared. Know what they are looking for and about the company or position you are interviewing for. Dress appropriately and be professional!"

MY FIRST APARTMENT

"I was living in a tiny apartment in a house in Saint Croix. No car, got to work by walking, running, or riding my bike! There were lots of cockroaches, no real oven, but the view was spectacular! I could walk across the road to a beach, snorkel a half-mile offshore to a reef, and catch lobster for dinner. The hotel guests across the road always looked at me like I was crazy."

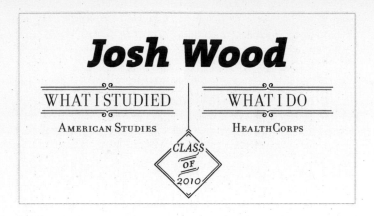

Josh Wood

WHAT I STUDIED	WHAT I DO
AMERICAN STUDIES	HEALTHCORPS

CLASS OF 2010

"Be less worried. Senior year in college is a once-in-a-lifetime opportunity."

Josh had always been interested in community service and the environment, so he had a general idea of the type of job he wanted after graduation. As a freshman, he had wanted to be a geology researcher, but he changed his mind when the time came to declare a major. "I switched majors because I thought geology was a little too concentrated. I wanted something broader, thinking it would enable me to apply to more jobs," he said.

After applying to everything he was interested in by March of his senior year, Josh was rather relaxed for the latter part of his second semester, as all he could do was wait. He began to attend seminars and participate in one-on-one meetings at his college career center, which he believes aided him in his job interviews.

During his last semester, Josh realized that he would have his whole life to apply for a job, but had only a limited amount of time to spend with friends. He wanted to take advantage of living close to all of his friends, so he didn't spend all of his time searching for jobs.

After noticing a flyer posted in a dorm room, Josh learned about HealthCorps and Green Corps, non-profits centered on education and mentoring in school systems and environmental organizing, respectively. Each organization coincided with his beliefs and what he wanted to do with his life after graduation. Two weeks before he finished school, Josh accepted a position with HealthCorps as a health teacher at a middle school in New Jersey.

Senior Year Regrets:

"I would have used the alumni network a lot more. It seemed intimidating to reach out to alumni, yet I got a great internship over one summer through using it. Using the alumni network doesn't guarantee you a job, but it can get you straight to the interview stage, which is really important."

What College Taught Me:

"First and foremost, I have learned a lot about myself through college. I came out of high school thinking I knew so much about the world and myself, and boy, was I wrong. Learning to see new points of view, and perhaps most importantly, being open to learning in every way possible, especially experimentally, was incredible, and I wouldn't trade one day of my college [experience] for anything."

Life in the Real World:

"It's great! Well...it's not college. Working is hard. You can't say, 'Nah, I'm not in the mood to work; I'll go to the library in a few hours.' However, there isn't (much) homework, so when you are *off*, you are *off*. And it's certainly nice not to have to dread Sunday nights anymore. The transition to the real world the year after college is a difficult one, no matter what you are doing. I have found that attitude is key. You can't go back to college, but you are young and probably in a really cool city! You have energy and friends you won't have in a few decades—enjoy it!"

Advice for Graduates:

"Network using your university alumni! You get your foot in the door that way, and it is a much more efficient use of time than Idealist or Monster—everyone looks there. Have fun! Stay true to your ideals, and try to express them. Go see art, take in lectures, and talk with like-minded (and non-like-minded) people. Continue to keep the dialogue going, because the real world is where the dialogue actually matters."

WORDS OF WISDOM

"Three things are important to me post-college: hanging with friends, being happy, and having enough money for beer and rent (in that order)."

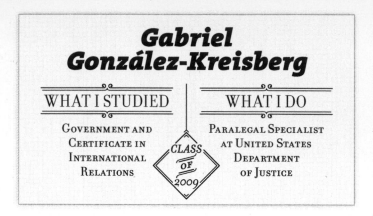

Gabriel González-Kreisberg

WHAT I STUDIED	WHAT I DO
GOVERNMENT AND CERTIFICATE IN INTERNATIONAL RELATIONS	PARALEGAL SPECIALIST AT UNITED STATES DEPARTMENT OF JUSTICE

CLASS OF 2009

"Always carry your drink and food in your left hand when you are at a reception. It leaves your right hand free to shake hands."

By using his college career center regularly during senior year, Gabriel was able to establish a strong and effective rapport with the staff. Throughout his four years in college, his dream was to move to Washington, D.C., and be a diplomat for the United States Department of State. He explored positions with the Department of Justice, amongst other branches of government, as he sought entry-level positions that could serve as a foundation for his career. Since he knew exactly what he wanted, Gabriel was not only able to receive more specific assistance with his job hunt, but was also very confident about what his future held. In his eyes, the last few months of college were left to hang out with friends and go to parties. Unfortunately, he graduated without a job offer and moved home to Amherst, Massachusetts, where he planned on staying for the summer to decompress and enjoy a last "true" summer.

Happy and resigned to the fact that he would be a college graduate without a job, Gabriel did not stress himself out over his uncertain future. There was no significant amount of pressure or anxiety, since he planned on giving himself a "buffer" by being at home for the summer and treating it like a vacation. Fortunately, in early June, he was contacted for an interview by Abt Associates, a political consulting firm that he had reached out to after speaking with alumni of his school's government department. Shortly after the interview, he was offered the position of associate with a start date in September, which he gladly accepted. A month later, he finally heard back from the Department of Justice and was asked to interview with them as well. He decided to resign from the consulting firm and accept the position with the Department of Justice.

"Each interview I went to, I printed out as much information about the company and the job and read and highlighted it all," he said. "I then sat down and wrote bulleted points comparing my internship, athletic, and college experience to what I had learned about the job/company. From that information, I was able to establish key points I would want to hit in my interview, sort of all-purpose answers that I would steer the interview toward. Besides that, I slept well and sat in an air-conditioned place and reviewed my notes before I interviewed."

Senior Year Regrets:
"I pretty much wouldn't change all that much, besides applying to more jobs. I applied to maybe four jobs that I really wanted, and got two, so I would have liked to explore my options more."

What College Taught Me:

"Networking is really important. Always carry your drink and food in your left hand when you are at a reception. It leaves your right hand free to shake hands. Do something you love and enjoy, because if you don't, then you aren't happy."

Life in the Real World:

"Get roommates you like. Or at least get ones that are smart. [Recently,] one of my roommates woke up my other roommate because he had left his room at 4:00 a.m. to go to the vending machine in our building, but didn't bring his key or his phone. This Harvard graduate managed to lock himself out of the house and banged on the door until my other roommate woke up. Good roommates are an invaluable part of living in the real world."

Advice for Graduates:

"Be relaxed, apply to things you really want to do, and really write a good cover letter that explains why you want to work somewhere, and why *they* should want *you* for their company. I've always found that having a personal stake in your work makes it more compelling."

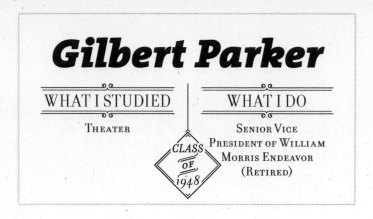

Gilbert Parker

WHAT I STUDIED

Theater

WHAT I DO

Senior Vice President of William Morris Endeavor (Retired)

CLASS OF 1948

"I knew I wanted to be an actor, but had no idea how to do it."

As a freshman, Gilbert had no clue what he wanted to do with his life, but his ambitions became clear after he took theater courses and developed a rapport with the chairman of the department. "My parents were horrified...because I wanted to go into acting," he said. After he completed his obligatory service in the Navy in 1945 (which interrupted his time in college), Gilbert graduated with a theater degree in 1948. Following graduation, he spent several months in Cleveland, where he worked seven days a week and ten hours a day.

"I got an internship at The Cleveland Playhouse. I was ushering, building sets; anything they wanted me to do, I did it," he said. After Cleveland, and at the recommendation of his mother, he explored the idea of becoming a teacher. "My mom kept saying, 'When the acting thing doesn't work out, you can teach,' and I said, 'If it doesn't work out.'" Gilbert applied to a teaching program in Washington, D.C., and also to Fordham University for a master's in theater, as he began to doubt earning a living being an actor.

With acceptances from both programs, Gilbert was conflicted as to which road to go down: the "safe" teaching route, or the acting route, which was a giant gamble. He chose to attend Fordham for theater. In his first year, he met a young woman at a party who got him a job as the switchboard operator at a literary agency. Six months later, he was asked to be the assistant to Aubrey Wood, the agent to Tennessee Williams, William Inge, and Robert Anderson. The job paid $30 a week.

Senior Year Regrets:

"I would do everything the same."

What College Taught Me:

"Feelings of dedication. I also learned that I wanted friends who were involved in the arts."

Life in the Real World:

"I lucked out. Joan Denny, [the woman] at the party, helped me out. I was open to anything. You have to be open to all opportunities presented to you."

Advice for Graduates:

"Get your foot in the door. If you want to be something, get an apprenticeship or internship, start hanging around, volunteering, etc. If there is an opening somewhere, you gotta be there."

MY FIRST APARTMENT

"When I lived in New York, I lived in a six-floor walkup. There was one bathroom and five bedrooms and no bathroom sink. There were people moving in and out every week. One time someone called and asked for Marilyn and I had no idea who she was or if she lived there, because there were new people all the time. The rent was $25 a month."

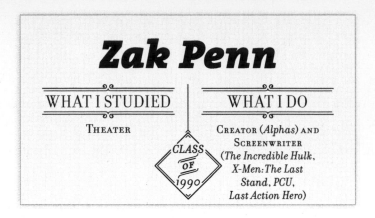

Zak Penn

WHAT I STUDIED

THEATER

CLASS OF 1990

WHAT I DO

CREATOR (*Alphas*) AND SCREENWRITER (*The Incredible Hulk*, *X-Men:The Last Stand*, *PCU*, *Last Action Hero*)

"I liked college a lot, but I couldn't wait to get started and start my career."

Growing up in New York and idolizing Woody Allen, Zak had been a playwright most of his young adult life. As a freshman, he knew that he wanted to work in Hollywood once he graduated. He decided to forgo the traditional study abroad format in another country and instead took classes at the University of Southern California for a semester in his junior year to familiarize himself with the entertainment industry. When graduation came, he was excited instead of anxious or nervous. "A bunch of my classmates were moving out to Los Angeles, and so was my girlfriend [now wife]. I lived with them in a cheap, crappy apartment and began writing," he said.

Looking for ways to pay his rent while he worked on his passion, Zak was introduced to a woman through a family friend; she paid him to take care of her household chores. "When I got out to Los Angeles, I got a job feeding this lady's cat and taking out her garbage. Then a friend got me a job reading scripts and writing covers [summaries of the script]. If they like what you write, you read more. I started doing more script reading and some researching." He was then hired as a script reader, where the main emphasis was on one's writing experience and skill. "I really never had to do all that much of an interview and go through the process. It was all about writing samples."

After fourteen months of learning the business, writing every day, and feeding cats, Zak and his writing partner, Adam Leff, got an agent and sold their first script, *Last Action Hero*.

Senior Year Regrets:
"Nothing. I think it all worked out all right."

What College Taught Me:
"College was an opportunity to have a really good time. If you are interested in the arts, particularly writing, it's an excellent opportunity to write without having normal pressures. College is an opportunity to practice one's craft. One has the opportunity to exercise their creative muscles in safety, with room to develop. Don't underestimate being around peers who are writing and acting. You can help each other, just like [how] with sports, if you want to be a pro baseball player, you want to be around other baseball players."

Life in the Real World:
"It's a bit of a shock. Cars and insurance and rent are issues that college doesn't prepare you for, so get it right."

Advice for Graduates:
"Don't count on being as lucky as I was. It is a good idea to get a sense of what you want to do. Going out to Los Angeles a year

and a half before [graduation] was probably a smart move. I knew that is what I wanted to do, so that prepped me. Whatever you can do to prepare yourself is helpful. Figure out something you enjoy doing and find a way to get paid doing it. Enjoy it and don't worry about it.

"You end up doing something that is either familiar or makes a lot of money, and the problem is you get stuck. Lots of people have this false vision that lightning will strike and tell you 'This is what you should do.' Use college as an opportunity to figure out what you like and dislike."

DISASTROUS INTERVIEW

"Early on, when I was trying to meet people to get a leg up in the business, I was a notoriously late sleeper. I never took classes in college that started before 1:00 p.m. But this was the real world and the real world has real hours. I had a meeting scheduled for 9:00 a.m. and figured I would need coffee for it. I had never drunk coffee before. But I was supposed to meet this guy for advice, and I drank two cups of coffee. When I met with him and sat down he said, 'I don't know what it was like in college, but you can't do cocaine and meet people in the real world.' Don't pick interview [times] early in the morning if you can't make it."

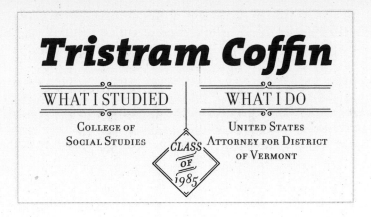

Tristram Coffin

WHAT I STUDIED

COLLEGE OF
SOCIAL STUDIES

CLASS OF 1985

WHAT I DO

UNITED STATES
ATTORNEY FOR DISTRICT
OF VERMONT

"Remember, there is no dress rehearsal; you're on, so enjoy it and go for it. Don't be afraid to take some chances."

In his senior year, Tristram was wrapped up in managing his life at school and didn't focus on the next steps. "For better or for worse, I was into school itself, my thesis, friends, fun, and rowing," he said. With a loose plan to pursue either academia or law, he didn't decide on anything before graduation. He moved to Somerville, Massachusetts, once he graduated. He got a job in a boat supplies store through a friend and gave sailing lessons on the Boston Harbor.

"I was living in an apartment outside of Boston and driving an old Jeep Cherokee. I had a lot of fun and made the princely sum of five dollars an hour, a wage I was moderately excited about, but not much of a future," he said. Tristram's girlfriend at the time lived in New York and was very driven and career-oriented, which only magnified Tristram's situation and led him to question his own path.

"I would visit her, feeling very lame, as she would go off to work each day at a high-powered career-track job. After a few days,

I decided I needed to do something about this. I put on a suit and went building to building in Lower Manhattan passing out résumés at big law firms. So after a couple of days, I had three job offers for paralegal jobs. Not quite 'Master of the Universe' stuff, but it would pay the bills."

Senior Year Regrets:

"While it is obviously important, don't put too much stock in your career. These days, things are not fully in one's control. There is much, much more to life than your job. Be nice and try to help others."

What College Taught Me:

"Don't stress too much about time. You certainly don't want to waste it, but as you come out of school you actually do have a long time ahead of you. It might take time to find the right thing, or if you have found it, to work your way into your career path and get on the road or get established."

Life in the Real World:

"Don't be afraid of change. Embrace it. I've made some pretty big changes in my career and they have been really refreshing and fun."

Advice for Graduates:

"Find the right thing and be confident about that. You'll know it when you find it. Being a bit tough and thick-skinned is really important and goes a long way. Smile, but be persistent and direct your own plan."

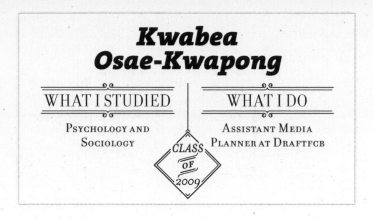

Kwabea Osae-Kwapong

WHAT I STUDIED	WHAT I DO
PSYCHOLOGY AND SOCIOLOGY	ASSISTANT MEDIA PLANNER AT DRAFTFCB

CLASS OF 2009

"It's an interesting situation to be gone for four years, living on your own, and then suddenly you are back living with your parents."

As a freshman in college, Kwabea had no clue what she wanted to be or do once she graduated. Only after an amazing summer internship in advertising before her senior year did she realize that she wanted to go into the field. In her last semester, as her friends and peers began accepting job offers, she became nervous about her life after college. "Graduating was scary! The job I really wanted wasn't available to me [assistant account executive], which got incredibly frustrating because I didn't have enough experience. I was sad that school was ending, but equally as excited to start that next chapter."

After graduation, Kwabea began interning with an advertising company she found online. The combination of living at home and working as an intern became taxing for her; her life was not going according to plan. "I wanted to be able to have a job once September came around, and instead I was an intern," she said. "I was discouraged because I had thought that I would have a permanent job with a salary two to three months out of college and I would be living on my own."

While she received her internship through a website, Kwabea landed her full-time job through a connection with a friend. "I reached out to a fellow intern from the program I did the summer before senior year and they forwarded my résumé to their [current company's] Human Resources department. That was my in." A day after her interview, Kwabea was offered the position of Assistant Media Planner at Draftfcb. "Now, it's about trying to get promoted and moving forward," she added.

Senior Year Regrets:

"Nothing. Rather than doing nothing when I couldn't get a job, I took an intern position just to get the experience while I could to boost my résumé."

What College Taught Me:

"The real world is so much different than college. I wish I would have stressed less and just had more fun with my friends and boyfriend. In college, you have more free time than you realize. Even if you don't graduate with a job, enjoy everything you can about college, and everything ends up pretty good once you graduate."

Life in the Real World:

"Being in the real world is difficult! There's a lot more responsibility, especially if your parents stop supporting you once you graduate."

Advice for Graduates:

"I was definitely given a reality check that it is not the easiest thing in the world to graduate and then end up with the dream job you want. I would suggest that if you're having a tough time finding a job, take an internship position if possible. While you might not be making the money you want to be, you'll be able to get experience and enhance your résumé. If you can't find an internship position to take, consider working in a field that might be slightly different than what you want, but has job responsibilities similar to the job you want.

"You may not get the job you want right away, but don't give up on it if it's something you really want. Things will change and an opportunity will come your way when it's meant to. In the meantime, do whatever you can to help yourself move forward in the right direction toward that dream job. In the end, you may decide that it's not the job you really wanted, but at least you'll know you did everything you could to get yourself there."

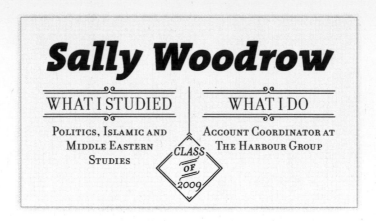

Sally Woodrow

WHAT I STUDIED | **WHAT I DO**

Politics, Islamic and Middle Eastern Studies | Account Coordinator at The Harbour Group

CLASS OF 2009

"I graduated without knowing what my future plans were."

Sally felt that her dance classes and thesis were taking up her entire life as a senior, so she was not able to dedicate enough time to searching for and applying to jobs. "I would have certainly preferred to have things figured out prior to graduation, but after a while decided I needed to resolve the situation when I was finished with my school commitments," she said.

Sally had an offer to teach dance at a local high school and had been accepted into a B.A./M.A. program in Islamic and Middle Eastern Studies at the college she attended as an undergrad, but she found herself thinking that if she became a teacher, it would be a choice based on convenience rather than genuine desire. "I knew that if I went that route, I would feel as though I was taking the easy way out instead of chasing after what I really wanted, which was to move to D.C. and pursue politics."

With dreams of being Secretary of State or moving home to California, Sally knew that she had to make a big choice upon graduating. She decided to move to Washington, D.C., without a job, which left her feeling anxious, but also with a sense of determination and purpose.

"I used any and all resources I had access to in my job search," she said. "My most successful finds came from personal networking or networking through my school's alumni database. The position I ultimately took was not posted online anywhere. Rather, I did some networking with a casual friend/acquaintance. She had previously worked under the Managing Director of the public relations firm I ended up working for. She sent in my résumé after she realized the intersection of our interests (Middle East focus) and I was called in for an interview a few weeks later."

Senior Year Regrets:

"I think that much of a job search is up to fate—it's all about being in the right place at the right time. I suppose I could have started the networking process earlier, but the most important thing is to be physically present in the city you want to be in, so you can jump on opportunities as quickly as possible."

What College Taught Me:

"Spend time developing relationships—classes are only part of what being a college student is about. Take advantage of the access you have to your professors."

Life in the Real World:

"Appearances and social skills go a long way. You may be overqualified for a job, but if you don't have chemistry with your co-workers, you surely won't get the position. Know how to socialize and find common ground with whomever you meet. Also, age is just a number. You need to learn how to interact and hold your own among people decades older than you. When in a job, make sure you know how to advocate for yourself. Be diligent about your work, but also be sure to be clear with your supervisors about what kind of projects you'd like to work on. Take initiative, or else they will assign you to whatever is most convenient for them. It is more important for your long-term professional development to take on new tasks and diversify your experiences than master one or two areas."

Advice for Graduates:

"Try and focus as early as possible on what you want to do after you graduate, and build up a string of jobs, internships, and academic work that supports that statement. Take advantage of your school's career center and meet with them frequently throughout college. Have a very open mind about what your first job will be."

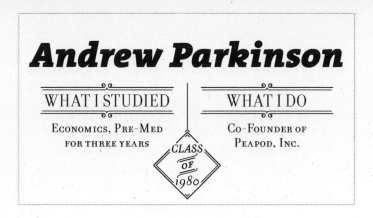

Andrew Parkinson

WHAT I STUDIED	WHAT I DO
Economics, Pre-Med for three years	Co-Founder of Peapod, Inc.

CLASS OF 1980

"Never met a party I didn't enjoy!"

When he was a junior, Andrew decided to stop fulfilling his pre-med requirements and pursue business, since he and his brother had been very successful as entrepreneurs on campus, where they had sold T-shirts and other products. He relied heavily on his college's career resource center and set up interviews with J.P. Morgan, Chemical Bank, and Procter & Gamble. "I was pretty focused on finding a job, as I knew I would have to support myself and pay back my student loans once I graduated," he said. "I was also pretty sure my parents didn't want me hanging out at home with nothing to do, so I was motivated."

Both sad and excited about college ending, Andrew was anxious to start working in the business world. Like his brother Thomas (pages 61-62), he didn't have any capital for his business ideas. Therefore, they both sought out large companies in the hopes of learning as much as possible, so they would be able to start their own business later on.

"I worked at Procter & Gamble, and then Kraft Foods, in Brand Management. That helped me understand the workings of the business world, as well as provided some credibility for raising money when my brother and I started Peapod."

When Andrew was working for Procter & Gamble, he came across a study that said seventy percent of consumers dislike shopping for groceries. Around the same time, the use and popularity of computers were beginning to increase, and Andrew thought about bringing the two—the convenience of computers and consumers' dislike of grocery shopping—together. "I thought to myself, 'If I could solve the problem of people disliking grocery shopping with computers, I could have something,'" he said.

He teamed up with his brother to form a business plan, and strategy became the top priority as each used the skills and resources from their previous work experiences to build their own company. They founded Peapod, a grocery delivery company that provides customers with both the website to order food from and the delivery service of whatever they choose to order.

The brothers' desire to start their own business was based on the success and ingenuity of a creation of theirs from college called the Keg Karrier: a three-foot-round metal bar with bicycle grips at either end and a set of prongs that would grab both ends of a beer keg to help carry it up and down stairs.

Senior Year Regrets:
"The key thing for me was that I took advantage of the college career resource center to get interviews."

What College Taught Me:
"I made great friends that I am in touch with today, learned about

the benefit of hard work and persistence, and the importance of always being honest with yourself and others."

Life in the Real World:

"Never give up, be persistent, be honest, and you will do well, whether in finding a job or doing well at the job you find."

Advice for Graduates:

"First off, I would advise working during the summer so that you can demonstrate your willingness to work hard at whatever job you do. Employers want to hire people who show initiative. Secondly, I would take advantage of your college's career resource center. It is an excellent way to learn about potential opportunities that might interest you, as well as to line up interviews. Lastly, whatever you wind up doing, work hard and never give up. You'll have up and down days, but if you can push through the down days, you'll come out on top and, hopefully, enjoying what you do. Hard work, persistence, integrity, and belief in oneself are what I look for in good employees at our company today."

DISASTROUS INTERVIEW

"I was interviewing with an econometrics company, and I spent twenty minutes telling the interviewer all about our Keg Karrier business and how we had sold it to fraternities all around the country. He seemed very engaged and interested, but he said, 'I don't understand why you need a special device for two guys to carry a cake.' When I told him I had been talking about a 'keg' carrier and not a 'cake' carrier, the gentleman burst out laughing and miraculously launched a long piece of snot that landed on his knee, but was still attached to his nose, apparently without real-izing it. So there I was, trying to look earnestly at this guy who had a long strand of snot stringing from his nose to his knee, while he talked for another five minutes as if nothing was unusual. I'm not sure he ever did figure it out. In any case, my gross-out factor was sufficient that I didn't want the job by the time the interview was over, which didn't matter much since they never offered me the job anyway."

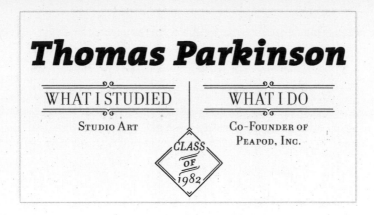

Thomas Parkinson

WHAT I STUDIED | **WHAT I DO**

STUDIO ART | CO-FOUNDER OF
PEAPOD, INC.

CLASS OF 1982

"I was extremely anxious as I approached graduation. Who am I? What am I doing?"

With graduating approaching, Thomas realized that a career as an artist would likely not result in very much income. As an entrepreneur throughout college, he made money on the side by selling t-shirts and Keg Karriers, an invention he and his brother Andrew (pages 57-60) created. By senior year, however, he also began to realize that being an entrepreneur right out of college was almost impossible, since he had no money to start anything. He decided it was best to work with a big company where he could learn some business skills, so he interviewed for a marketing position, as well as a sales position, with Proctor & Gamble. "I totally screwed up on the marketing interview because my educational background didn't match the job," he said. "The interview for sales went really well, as my personality and sales skills were the right fit."

After accepting the job, Thomas moved to Syracuse, New York, where he worked extremely hard all the time and learned as much as he could, which propelled him on the path of starting his own business.

Senior Year Regrets:

"Nothing."

What College Taught Me:

"College made me very independent and resourceful. It also gave me an unbelievable amount of best friends that have supported me to this day."

Life in the Real World:

"If I knew then what I know now, I wouldn't have been so afraid. You find out that you are just as capable as everyone else, if not more so."

Advice for Graduates:

"Don't worry so much about your first job. Just take one. Then see where life leads you."

"When I moved to New York City I lived on a couch at a friend's apartment. Then I found a four-month rental in a disgusting Upper East Side railroad apartment with the bathtub in the kitchen. I finally found a place with two other roommates on the Upper West Side. I was a nomad in New York City, but was having the time of my life."

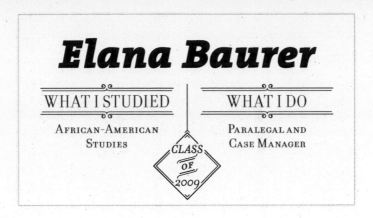

Elana Baurer

WHAT I STUDIED

African-American
Studies

CLASS OF 2009

WHAT I DO

Paralegal and
Case Manager

"I tried to form an articulate spiel about where I was coming from and what my motivation was for doing social justice work."

When Elana started college, she thought she might be interested in doing policy work once she graduated. During her senior year and after a summer internship at the Women's Law Project in Philadelphia, she was convinced she wanted to become a lawyer. Throughout her life, she had been involved in the Jewish community in various capacities, such as teaching at synagogues, tutoring Hebrew, and taking religion/Jewish classes in college. She ended up using her interest in Judaism as a means to assist her in the process of getting jobs before she attended law school.

"I started the application process early. Because I knew how difficult the job market would be, I started looking at programs like AmeriCorps, Jewish service programs, and labor organizing developed particularly for young people that provide training and support. I was accepted to AVODAH: The Jewish Service Corps in March of my senior year."

A week after her acceptance, she interviewed with three organizations through AVODAH and accepted an offer to work at the

New York Legal Assistance Group as a paralegal and case manager.

As Elana was getting a jump-start on her career, she was also coming to terms with the fact that college was ending. Since she had lots of plans in motion and there was minimal uncertainty, she was more eager than fearful for the next phase. "At the end of senior year I was feeling anxious about the next step, although excited to be living in New York with so many friends."

Senior Year Regrets:

"Nothing. I'm happy with the path I took."

What College Taught Me:

"I learned how to challenge myself without overwhelming myself, both in relationships and academically."

Life in the Real World:

"I learned how to live on $320 a month. That was my stipend at AVODAH. Buying communally saves money, and never drinking coffee out saves a lot, too."

Advice for Graduates:

"Use connections and also try to go through alumni networks; I know a lot of people who get help from that. Also, be patient and give yourself six months. Don't be discouraged by not getting interviews and rejection and see every application and interview as a learning experience."

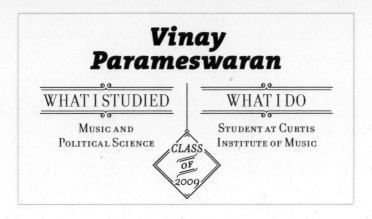

Vinay Parameswaran

WHAT I STUDIED

Music and
Political Science

CLASS OF 2009

WHAT I DO

Student at Curtis
Institute of Music

"I put all of my eggs into the music school basket."

Even though Vinay had been a standout musician in high school, as a freshman in college he had thoughts of becoming a lawyer. It wasn't until halfway through his junior year that he decided to seriously and actively pursue a career in music. "My thoughts were, 'I need to get into a school!' I didn't really have much of a backup plan; thus I applied to over ten schools," he said.

The idea of switching from a potential law degree to a music degree is perceived, by some, to be a significant gamble, one that can potentially be very challenging and discouraging. For Vinay, it felt right. "I was somewhat sad that school was ending, but excited about coming to Curtis. I was excited to move to Philadelphia and that some of my closest friends were going to be here as well."

Originally trained as a classical pianist and percussionist, Vinay's sole focus is now classical music and conducting. Although he does not have a specific city or country in mind, he hopes to have a career working with various orchestras and opera companies around the world. He is, however, resigned to the fact that he is going to start at the bottom and have to work his way up. "Ideally, I'll start as an Assistant Conductor with an orchestra, where I'll learn and work under that orchestra's music director (who is the principal conductor), and then after a few years, hopefully I'll be able to land a Music Director job of my own."

Senior Year Regrets:

"Nothing, really. Applying to and going to [Curtis Institute of Music] is the best thing for me."

What College Taught Me:

"How to think creatively, the value of relationships (with anyone), how to speak publicly, to really do what you love."

Life in the Real World:

"I don't know what to make of it, but I know it's going to be tough."

Advice for Graduates:

"While it may not be ideal, take anything you can get, considering the economic circumstances. It's great to be idealistic, but everyone has to start small, and it's best to grab any opportunity that comes along. Spend as much time with your close friends as possible, and take advantage of everything that your school offers."

Bill Sherman

WHAT I STUDIED	WHAT I DO
Music	Composer *(In the Heights)*

CLASS OF 2002

"I got a job in a diner flipping burgers and making milkshakes."

While in his senior year, Bill decided it best to concentrate on his thesis and final concert and to just have a good time playing music. He was not ready to leave college, but realized he had no control over the situation; his time as a student was up, and he chose to make the best of it by focusing on his music without worrying about what came next. "Entering college, I wanted to be a jazz saxophone player with as much worldly music knowledge as I could find. Leaving, I had no idea what I was going to do," he said.

"I didn't foresee any post-graduate schooling for myself, so I knew that this would be the last time I was in school. I was surely anxious to see what was next. I had a music degree from a liberal arts school and had spent much of my collegiate career playing West African music and conducting music theater pieces. Jobs in these fields are difficult, if not impossible, to come by, so I was surely a little worried about what lay ahead in my field."

After graduation, and with no discernable options, Bill moved in with his parents in rural Western Massachusetts. "It was a good way to decompress from college and figure out my next move."

Fortunately for Bill, a friend's father was a "higher up" at Viacom, which runs MTV. As he wanted to live in New York and take his musical background to the next level, Bill sought an interview and jumped at the opportunity when one was offered.

"In the interview process, I always felt like it was important to be as knowledgeable about the place you were interviewing as possible. That, and the willingness to say yes to just about anything. When you're trying to find that first work experience, and you need money to move out and make a name for yourself, you are willing to do and say whatever it takes to get the job," he said.

Once Bill was offered the job as a paid intern in the IT department, he moved to the Inwood neighborhood of Manhattan with Lin-Manuel Miranda (creator, writer, and lead of *In the Heights*). "Having the opportunity to live with my close friends in an environment that was financially manageable was a dream come true. While the living conditions were sometimes difficult (leaky ceilings, etc.), the freedom associated with moving out and being financially independent was well worth the hardships."

Senior Year Regrets:

"I think I would have thought about it much sooner and taken some steps to explore some other opportunities through college. I know a number of graduates who were able to locate jobs in their respective fields through the career resource center."

What College Taught Me:

"I always say that what I do now, from a very practical standpoint, is not something I learned specifically in college. I will say that college was a place to network and make connections with an unbelievably intelligent and motivated group of people who, in my case, would impact and change my life forever. Also, college is an environment for trying new things (classes, politics, etc.) and seeing how they pan out as opposed to overthinking them from the get-go and deciding to not ever try them at all. As you mature, finding environments like that is difficult."

Life in the Real World:

"It is difficult. Also, putting yourself in the right place at the right time is as important as being good at what you do. Finally, at a certain point, everyone vying for a particular job has a similar set of skills. It then becomes a case of whether or not you are a person that people want to have around. That is an important thing to know."

Advice for Graduates:

"In the beginning, say yes to everything. You never know what opportunities will arise from an experience you put yourself in by saying yes to it, even if it seemed questionable from the onset."

RAMEN AND PIZZA

"Living on ramen noodles and pizza bagels and struggling to get by is a real thing. I will say that it certainly helped me understand the importance of providing for yourself and being responsible with what you got. That, and never losing sight of your dreams. Ever. If you can see yourself there, you can get there."

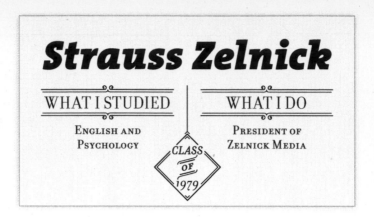

Strauss Zelnick

WHAT I STUDIED
ENGLISH AND
PSYCHOLOGY

CLASS OF 1979

WHAT I DO
PRESIDENT OF
ZELNICK MEDIA

"Narrow down your goals. To get what you want, know what you want."

Strauss didn't think he'd get a job straight out of college, so he set his sights on graduate school with the idea that he would be in a better position for work if he had another degree or two. "I was sad school was ending. I always loved being in an academic environment and wanted that to continue. Things were only getting better, so I wanted to stay in school," he said.

Four months after graduating, Strauss was enrolled as a graduate student to earn both J.D. and M.B.A. degrees. As a joint law and business student, he used the alumni networks from both programs as well as all of the other resources available to him to find employment opportunities. "There were a lot of recruiters who came to campus and I met with some of them, but I managed to get my summer job through a friend of a friend at Viacom," he said. The summer position was with Columbia Pictures in international television sales and proved to be a significant steppingstone, as it launched his career in business and media.

Senior Year Regrets:

"Would have been more organized about the search. Done more homework."

What College Taught Me:

"Everyone starts in same place. Some have family money and history. But everyone starts in the same place in terms of building a career. Assuming you don't want to be given something, everyone starts from scratch."

Life in the Real World:

"First thing that was different was that I didn't take time off. There is less free time. Even in grad school I had evenings free. In school you have summers off. Out here you have two weeks of vacation. It's a real shift from college life. It's not a bad idea to take time [off] from college and grad school or college and whatever you do next."

Advice for Graduates:

"Make sure you figure out what you want. Narrow down your goals. To get what you want, know what you want. Think realistically about your goals and make sure they are constant with your values. Be honest with yourself. Persevere and know that it might not happen quickly or it might not happen at all. Really understand the nature of the business you are trying to get into. Reach out to people. Reach out to your alumni network."

Kevin Williams

WHAT I STUDIED

ECONOMICS, MINOR IN
COMPUTER SCIENCE

CLASS
OF
2009

WHAT I DO

GRADUATE STUDENT IN
ECONOMICS

"If college were eight years long, I would have been happy."

A serious college athlete, Kevin lived by the motto, "Eat, train, love." Even though he spent his senior year training daily, he and his track and field teammates narrowly avoided qualifying for Nationals on the day before graduation. "I really didn't party as much at the end of college as I'd anticipated because of [the training]," he said.

Throughout his time in college, Kevin had a strong interest in becoming a teacher. He had always wanted to teach. Before senior year, he was looking into working in high schools as well as programs like Teach For America, but the more he looked into it, the more his interest faded. "By senior year I didn't bother applying for Teach For America. It seems like a program designed to burn people out on teaching."

During his senior year, Kevin had a professor with whom he worked very closely on his senior essay; the professor encouraged him to go on to graduate school. "Applications involve a standardized test (in my case, the GRE), essays, faculty recommendations, and a bunch of other paperwork. There was no way

I was pulling that off during fall semester of my senior year." He wanted a break between college and graduate school, so he sought a job in technology, since the industry was booming and he had some computer science experience. "Through the career services at my school, I found a job posting that was clearly posted by an alum at a startup who had only contacted his alma mater as a gesture of good faith, so I ended up applying for it," he said. After submitting his résumé, Kevin had a phone interview, which led to an in-person interview and, finally, a job offer.

"That first winter felt too soon to consider graduate school," he said. "By winter of 2009, I was ready to go back to school. I'd been at my job for a year and a half, the company was awesome, but there wasn't any job at the company—that I was qualified for—that I could see myself doing long term. Now I'm in a Ph.D. program that will hopefully lend itself to getting a teaching/professor job where I can see myself staying and building a reputation."

Senior Year Regrets:

"I was staunchly against the big college recruiting companies like Teach For America, Deloitte, Mercer, etc. I didn't want to be a cog in a giant corporate machine. In retrospect, I shouldn't have been so idealistic. Yes, my friends that got those jobs are pawns, but they know it and, rightfully, don't care. They have gotten to meet a ton of great people, and those huge companies know how to give real responsibility to new hires. I ended up getting a software job through a family friend at the last minute by somewhat of a fluke after deciding to apply to grad schools and not teaching jobs."

What College Taught Me:

"Research, research, research before you spend any money on a company you need to fly out to interview with, and research anything you are unsure about."

Life in the Real World:

"I was amazed at how much money I spent. I actually lived at home my first year out of college with free rent and free dinners when I so desired. My credit card bill was basically just food and drinks, with the occasional vacation cash thrown in, and I still managed to spend most of what I was making. I think it's totally true that people give themselves a savings goal and then will spend up to that goal, regardless of circumstance, often frivolously. The higher you're willing to set that goal, the better.

"It's also comforting to know that pretty much everyone understands that your education is useless. Where you went to school matters for getting looked at, what you did in school can help ace the interview, but once you start the job, it's assumed that you're starting from square one."

Advice for Graduates:

"Talk to as many people as you can and try to focus on a city or two. That way, when you do talk to people, you can tell them where you want to be. When you ask Uncle Johnny, 'Hey, know anywhere I can get a job?' you're working against the human brain. We aren't wired to keep an index of available job opportunities for college grads. We are better equipped to index which of our friends live in which cities. If you ask Uncle Johnny, 'Know anyone in Chicago?' you'll give yourself a better chance by narrowing the focus. It's not what you know or whom you know; it's both, with a solid dose of luck thrown in."

Troy Cosey

WHAT I STUDIED

MARKETING AND
INTERNATIONAL
BUSINESS

CLASS OF 2010

WHAT I DO

BUSINESS ANALYST AT
TARGET CORP.

"Job interview preparation was very time consuming; it was like I was taking a whole other class."

Even though he had always wanted to work in a corporate environment, Troy questioned his career path and decisions as he entered senior year. All of the classes he took, as well as the summer internships he had, were part of a larger plan to get a corporate job offer once he graduated.

"There was definitely a point senior year [when] I was unsure if corporate is really where I wanted to be. I really contemplated other professions, such as teaching and sports management," he said.

Sad that school was ending, Troy welcomed having responsibilities and being completely financially and physically independent from anyone else. Therefore, he decided to accept a job offer from Target in his second semester, as the security, independence, and sense of accomplishment and pride in a job offer felt too good to pass up.

Senior Year Regrets:

"I wouldn't have self-selected with some of the bigger companies I was interested in."

What College Taught Me:

"Getting involved on campus is the single best way to help your cause in the job market, but also to better your community. Ask yourself how you want to leave your legacy."

Life in the Real World:

"Companies have all the power, especially in a rough economy. Humble yourself and fight through rejection."

Advice for Graduates:

"Start early and don't get discouraged by rejection. Enjoy the last few weeks of college."

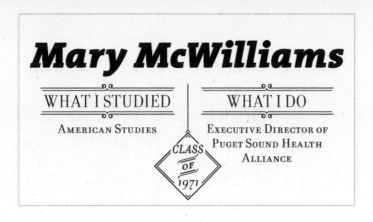

Mary McWilliams

WHAT I STUDIED	WHAT I DO
AMERICAN STUDIES	EXECUTIVE DIRECTOR OF PUGET SOUND HEALTH ALLIANCE

CLASS OF 1971

"Speak up for yourself in making your aspirations known."

Mary spent her summers off from high school and college working as a candy striper and in the admitting office at a teaching hospital. Shortly after transferring to another college in her junior year, she began to seriously contemplate a career in hospital administration. "The only challenges [about transferring] were limited athletic facilities and men who were more used to dating girls from other schools rather than on campus," she said. She took a traditional approach and elected to go to graduate school right after graduating, enrolling at the University of Colorado. which proved to be the foundation for her career.

"I was recommended for my first job as Marketing Director with the Rocky Mountain HMO by the head of my graduate program at the University of Colorado," she said. "The Executive Director of the company was a graduate of the same program I was in and HMOs were new, so no one knew very much. I took the job on the recommendation of a doctor in St. Louis, who said I had the chance to get in on the [ground] floor of a new approach to health care."

Senior Year Regrets:

"I was very lucky regarding grad school and my first job thereafter, so I wouldn't change a thing."

What College Taught Me:

"I learned about diversity [as an undergraduate]. I also observed that at 4:00 p.m. the men played pickup basketball and the women took a nap. So I decided that I needed to exercise every day instead, and I've held that commitment to this day."

Life in the Real World:

Take advantage of opportunities, but don't wait for them to be delivered to you. Your interpersonal skills are more important than your intellect."

Advice for Graduates:

"Go for the new, the unexplored, the cutting edge in the field in which you're interested. Work for someone who will be a mentor for you."

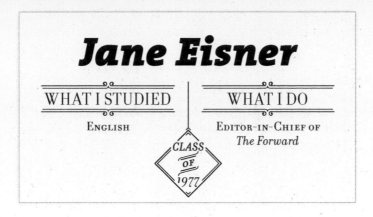

Jane Eisner

WHAT I STUDIED	WHAT I DO
ENGLISH	EDITOR-IN-CHIEF OF *The Forward*

CLASS OF 1977

"I was really, really focused during my first semester of senior year."

Jane had an extremely unique senior year; not only did she graduate a semester early, but she also received a job offer. "I had decided sometime in the fall that I wanted to audit some classes in the spring, but since I had enough credits and wanted to save money, it seemed best to graduate early and look for a job," she said. Using her former colleagues (from a summer position before senior year) as contacts and references, Jane applied for a part-time position with *The Hartford Courant*. "I got a call in December saying I got the job, but they now wanted me to be full time. I think it was because I told them I had a car during the interview. I didn't actually have a car."

While her classmates and friends were beginning their last semester in college, Jane began working the full-time newspaper position.

"I have mixed feelings about what I did. Part of me feels that I missed something by not having a regular second semester senior year. Didn't have the chance to take odd classes, to just hang out. I was thrown into a different social situation. I was interacting with those who were much older. I had one foot on campus, one foot off. I felt like I was in two separate worlds. It was awkward at times, but I was really grateful to earn the money. Friends didn't read *The Hartford Courant*. I still lived on campus with my friends, but it was a little weird going to work when they went to class."

About halfway through her job with the newspaper, Jane felt that she wanted to live in New York City and attend graduate school. She applied only to the Columbia School of Journalism, and she was accepted. This presented her with a very tough decision: go back to school and quit her full-time job or pass on school and remain employed. Contrary to what several people were advising her to do, she quit her job. "I backpacked and camped around with my husband (then boyfriend) throughout the country before grad school began in September. It all felt like the right thing to do."

Senior Year Regrets:

"I think that the opportunity to work was too good to pass up. I think that while it might have been unusual in how it materialized, instead of getting a job after [my] second semester, I got one after [my] first semester. Now, looking [back] and speaking with kids graduating, I feel that the pendulum has swung too far in the 'other' direction. There is not enough guidance for college students. No help to tailor their studies. It is such a tough job market out there that it's incumbent upon colleges and universities to do more."

What College Taught Me:

"So much. Well, it's where I grew up. College was a community to me. Part of my learning took place outside the classroom. I learned a lot by being the first woman editor of the school's newspaper. I learned that friendships don't always work out. I really learned a lot about Jewish life. I am still friends with the campus rabbi. I also noticed that I didn't stop learning once I graduated."

Life in the Real World:

"There is such a difference between college and the real world. The real world is...so much harder. Especially in terms of identity issues. I encountered a lot of obstacles. Much easier to blaze a trail in college than outside of it. There are a lot of social changes, too. In college, it's easy to know a lot of people and to feel like if you want to be part of a community, you can. The real world is less accepting, bigger, lonelier, but you gotta cope with it."

Advice for Graduates:

"Start thinking about life after college before you graduate. [It's] important to start to think about it midway through school, sophomore or junior year. I encourage [students] to think everything through. Completely. There are two main criteria. One, what is interesting to you? Two, will that thing be worthwhile [in a] bigger sphere (community, public, world)? Personally, I wanted to feel like I'm doing something to better someone or something. You need to look inward and outward. Don't just think through what will make you happy; what is something that is worthwhile where you can make some type of contribution? And just because you graduate, your relationship with the university doesn't have to end. You aren't restricted to friends, housemates, frat brothers, etc., and you can always reach back out to your school."

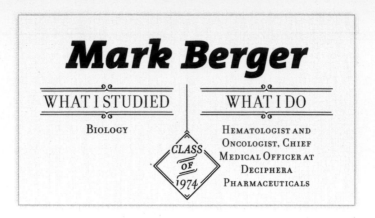

Mark Berger

WHAT I STUDIED

Biology

WHAT I DO

Hematologist and Oncologist, Chief Medical Officer at Deciphera Pharmaceuticals

CLASS OF 1974

"I spent several months picking grapefruits, and it made me feel good at the end of the picking day to see several crates of grapefruit that I'd picked—much more tangible an accomplishment than any paper I'd written."

Throughout college and even high school, Mark had always been a fan of the sciences, especially biology. In college, it wasn't a question of whether he would major in biology, but rather if he would go to graduate school or medical school afterwards. In the first and only semester of his senior year—Mark had enough credits to graduate without being enrolled for the entire year—he elected to apply to medical school, while also deciding to take the second semester off to save money and travel to Israel for a kibbutz program (a community where people live and work together on a non-competitive basis).

"It was a wonderful thing to have done," he said. "It put me in much better shape to go to medical school. I didn't study abroad, but this was part of the idea to make up for that. I wanted to save money. I wanted a non-academic experience. I thought it would take away some of the pressure feelings one has in school."

A couple of weeks before the program began, Mark received a letter of acceptance to medical school, leaving his time in Israel worry-free. While on the kibbutz, he spent several months picking fruit and working at a plant nursery, which gave him a sense of accomplishment while also preparing him for medical school.

"I spent several months picking grapefruits, and it made me feel good at the end of the picking day to see several crates of grapefruit that I'd picked—much more tangible an accomplishment than any paper I'd written. In brief, I chilled. And I needed that before moving on to medical school."

Mark returned to the United States to walk with his classmates for graduation and then moved in with his parents for the summer before medical school. "I made money and was able to save a bit since I lived at home, but I wouldn't recommend working a job you know is going to be boring if you know you won't get anything out of it," he said. "You should plan your summers ahead of time and find jobs you know you will like. Or you should travel."

Senior Year Regrets:

"I don't regret going off to Israel, but I do regret not taking more advantage of that summer after undergrad. I didn't think it through. Once you start going to medical school, there isn't any free time. Really ever again."

What College Taught Me:

"Forming close friendships was essential. It's incredibly important to have a variety of friends, particularly for med school individuals, so you don't find yourself doing the same thing with the same people."

Life in the Real World:

"It wasn't an easy transition. Med school doesn't teach you many things you need to know as far as taking care of patients. I wasn't really prepared to be an intern, and the economic ladder of med school and residency was a shock. I had an internship in Philadelphia and the New Jersey Turnpike toll collectors were making more money than me and they went on strike!"

Advice for Graduates:

"Professional school experience is really valuable. It's also just as valuable not to slip into the mold of professional training just for the sake of doing it. Try your best to find creative ways to use what you've learned. Don't always go for the standard. The way things are isn't the way they have to be."

MEDICAL SCHOOL TOUR

"When I was visiting med schools, I was on a private tour with a current student, and he took me to the morgue. He thought it was going to be empty but we walked in on the middle of an autopsy. That was a little much."

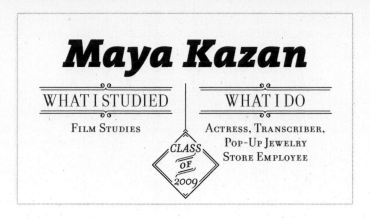

Maya Kazan

WHAT I STUDIED	WHAT I DO
FILM STUDIES	ACTRESS, TRANSCRIBER, POP-UP JEWELRY STORE EMPLOYEE

CLASS OF 2009

"Couple months after I graduated, I was really freaked out. I thought I would never get a job."

When Maya started college, she felt an extremely high level of pressure to excel in all facets of her college life, which ultimately led her to transfer.

"I think this pressure was mostly 'self-inflicted,' so to speak, but the culture of the school no doubt played a part. I don't know that I could say that it was the students or the professors, or the administration, but I was definitely not alone in feeling this kind of academic pressure. I think it is something that the school cultivates: a sense of responsibility, of obligation to take advantage of the privilege of studying...I felt like you weren't allowed to fail," she said. With a fresh start on a new campus, she realized that college is about trying new things and having the ability to make mistakes and learn from them without being judged.

Initially interested in publishing, Maya became more passionate about movies and directing once she began studying film. "I was good at reading and editing scripts and thought that working in theater in some capacity would be great," she said. During her senior year, she spent a great deal of time and resources on assisting her peers with their own thesis films, which left little time to focus on what she would do after graduation. "I wanted to figure it out, but I didn't have time to think about it because of the work I was doing, but also because I was so anxious about it that I just kept procrastinating," she said.

After graduating, Maya enrolled in an acting school, even though she wanted to become a director. "Initially I went into it backpedaling. I didn't know what else to do and it was just instinct. But then I felt that if you wanted to be a director and be in a position to tell actors what to do, what to say, where to go, you should know what they are doing. From their perspective." She shifted from directing to acting after she fell in love with her program and discovered a passion for the craft.

Senior Year Regrets:

"I would have used my career resource center at my school. I would have taken advantage of mental health options on campus to talk about how anxious I was."

What College Taught Me:

"I learned to accept myself in my failings and move forward. I learned that I don't have to be perfect; I can be a work in progress. I also learned how important it is to fail in college and to learn from those failings. Freshman year, I felt I wasn't allowed to fail, but once I transferred I was in a new atmosphere that let it be known it was okay to fuck up. I used to think that if I started on one path, I would never be able to get off it and try something else."

Life in the Real World:

"Nobody knows what they are doing or going to do in their twenties. When I was going into college, I thought everything would be figured out when I graduated, and nobody has it figured out."

Advice for Graduates:

"Don't be afraid to ask for help. Even from people who you think might not be able to help. If you are polite, and ask in a way that isn't entitled, people will help. People want to help young people. This is when you can get away with asking for help: after college. Use your window, man!"

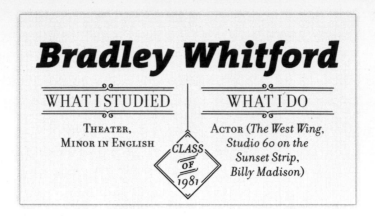

Bradley Whitford

WHAT I STUDIED	WHAT I DO
THEATER, MINOR IN ENGLISH	ACTOR (*The West Wing, Studio 60 on the Sunset Strip, Billy Madison*)

CLASS OF 1981

"You have a right, no matter what the economic pressures are, to do something you love."

Bradley spent senior year thinking about the future while trying to keep his anxiety to a minimum. "I remember being nervous during senior year in a way that I had never been before. I knew the kind of job I wanted [actor], but didn't know how it would work out," he said. Although waitlisted at Yale, he was accepted to Juilliard in January of his senior year. His last semester consisted of enjoying his friends and a lifestyle he knew could not be duplicated. "I was very sad school was ending, but I was excited to put on makeup and pretend to be someone else," he said. He knew he would be in massive debt by attending acting school, but he was passionate about continuing theater and moving to New York. "The 'stats' are really, really tough. We used to joke that Juilliard was med school with guaranteed unemployment at the end. You've got to be ready for that."

To Bradley, acting is a weird and tough business. It took some time, however, for him to realize most actors struggle and are constantly being rejected after auditions. Initially, he thought that when he graduated from acting school, he would be a paid actor. Of the thirty students in his acting class, twenty-two graduated and only three make a living from acting; none are women.

After graduating, he was working in the lunchroom at the World Trade Center, wondering if he had made the right choice by attempting to be an actor. After going through several auditions and experiencing firsthand how much rejection and struggle there is with acting, he was becoming very worried.

"Richard Schiff, who played Toby on *The West Wing*, is the brother of Paul Schiff, and he got me into auditions. Let me tell you, auditions are a nightmare. You have to do them *a lot*. It's very tricky because as an actor you are trying to access a kind of honesty and you have to do these psychological gymnastics to not react honestly. My metaphor for auditioning is that you go to a dog pound, here you have all these scared, homeless dogs in a strange environment. Reacting normally would make you cower and go to the back, but people pick the oblivious idiot in the front of the kennel. Preparation is relaxation. If you are really prepared, it will calm you down. When I do auditions, once I'm done, I am out the door. Beware the awkward lingering in show business."

One day, while serving sandwiches during lunch, Bradley received a phone call as a follow-up to his audition with an offer of a part in Sam Shepard's *Curse of the Starving Class* opposite Kathy Bates, and his immediate thought was, "Oh my God, what am I gonna do when this job is over?!"

What College Taught Me:

"I learned that there are several different types of people, and I'm always grateful for the diversity of interests and how that is celebrated in college. Idiosyncrasy was and should be celebrated."

Life in the Real World:

"It's never easy. There's a very specific thing about auditioning. For me, ninety percent of the time, I don't get the part. I can't control that. What I can control, if you are lucky enough to get an audition, is I can really prepare and have a really good acting experience for myself. I walk in assuming they aren't gonna give me the job. Instead of a failure, I see it as a learning experience."

Advice for Graduates:

"Really enjoy the end of college. Suck all the juice out of it. Think about what you will be best at, something you truly love and/or are interested in, and go for it. It's my experience, certainly in acting, and all the aspects of politics and show business and really everything, that there are very few tricks. It's all persistence. You're gonna have to deal with this. You're gonna run into a brick wall out there. Don't spend your precious time in that protected environment that it is such a privilege to be in by freaking out about the next year. You will put one foot in front of the other and figure it out. Try not to distract yourself too much. It's not make-or-break time. Far from it, actually. It's not like in your senior year, or even the first year after you graduate, you are entering a twelve-month period that will dictate your entire life. For anything, you need ten thousand hours of experience. Especially in something like acting. Actors can't all agree on one technique, so you just keep doing it until it works, or you change careers."

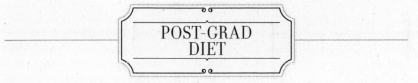

POST-GRAD
DIET

"Once I graduated, I ate a lot of ramen, yogurt, and peanut butter. No spoon. Straight finger into the jar."

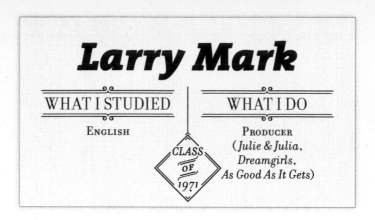

Larry Mark

WHAT I STUDIED	WHAT I DO
ENGLISH	PRODUCER (*Julie & Julia, Dreamgirls, As Good As It Gets*)

CLASS OF 1971

"Okay, what on Earth am I going to do now?!"

As far back as he can remember, Larry always had the entertainment industry on his mind. "I always wanted to be in film or theater," he said. "Or a big exec, or a producer, or director. Something in the business." As he complemented his English major with courses in film, he formed a relationship with a great professor, Jeannie Basinger, who suggested he look into graduate school. Prior to his acceptance to New York University's Tisch School for the Arts, he didn't necessarily have a fear of graduating, but he was, and admittedly still is, anxious about what comes next. "Sure, I'm almost always anxious for the next step," he said. "I was then and I am now. Even Meryl Streep is anxious for the next step, and she is Meryl Streep!"

In March of his second and final year in grad school, Larry decided he was going to look for a job and sent out five cold letters to professionals in the entertainment industry. As a result of his letters to film company presidents and award-winning producers, he was offered various internships and positions that ranged from touring with Maggie Smith as a production assistant to interning in the distribution department of Columbia Pictures. The best opportunity, however, came from David Picker.

"My roommate in college had season tickets to the New York Rangers," Larry explained. "I went to some games, and two seats down from us was David Picker, who was a big shot at United Artists and one of the individuals I wrote a letter to. So when I met with him, we had something to talk about, and that was my 'in.'"

Larry was hired by United Artists as an intern, which consisted of spending two to three weeks at the desk of each of the top executives of United Artists. This position propelled him into what he calls "the biz."

Senior Year Regrets:
"Nothing."

What College Taught Me:
"At school, one does learn the value of friendship. Much of your life is about who you get to hang out with. Including hanging out with professors. And here is the word I hesitate to use: NETWORKING."

Life in the Real World:
"I never differentiated the real world from school because I lived in New York for grad school. So even though I was living in a real city, I still had the buffer of school. I often recommend going to New York City after school."

Advice for Graduates:
"Write your own guidebook. First of all, if you follow someone else's, they are also following it. Don't be afraid to write your own.

There is no one way of getting somewhere. Keep your blinders on. Run your own race; don't be affected by your fellow classmate or colleague."

TWO JOB
OFFERS

"After I had been interning for a while at United Artists, David Picker, the man who hired me, left to produce a movie called *Lenny* with Dustin Hoffman. He offered me a position as an assistant on set, but the movie was filming in Miami and I didn't want to live in a rooming house in Miami. The original *Taking of Pelham One Two Three* was filming in New York and I interviewed with Steve Kesten, a producer, and he offered me a job working on that film. I loved New York and I didn't want to leave for Miami. Once Steve found out I had an opportunity to work with Dustin Hoffman and David Picker, he told me if I wanted to go somewhere in this industry, I should take that job. Here he was, telling me to take a job with another movie even though I wanted to work for him and he [had offered to hire me]. I ended up taking the job on *Lenny,* and that was some of the best advice I have ever gotten. Thanks to Steve Kesten!"

The
Roundabouts

THOSE WHO KNEW WHAT THEY WANTED,
BUT WENT BY PARTICULARLY
CIRCUITOUS ROUTES TO GET THERE.

Stephen Grodski

WHAT I STUDIED

Classics

WHAT I DO

Team Leader at
City Year New York

CLASS OF 2010

"I could go to school forever."

Once his last semester began, Stephen found himself rather upset that his college experience was coming to a close. "I was bummed out school was ending, just because I loved my major and the faculty within my department," he said. As a freshman, he had had no clue what he wanted to do after school, nor what he should study. He soon settled on a classics major after missing the deadline to register for classes and having to take an Ancient Greek History course. "It was my favorite class I ever took. I was doing my own supplemental reading and everything—I loved it. Being that it was the only topic of study I [had] enjoyed at college up to that point, I had no choice but to make it my major," he said.

By the time senior year rolled around, Stephen was thinking about law and graduate school programs while spending the majority of his time writing papers and studying. With his sights set on a classics graduate program in England, he spent a lot of his free time on his application and arranging recommendations. As it became clearer that the program was very selective and he would have a difficult time getting in, he turned his attention to getting a job in New York. "I had constantly conflicting attitudes and thoughts," he said. "I had an overwhelming fear of returning home to live with my parents sans job, so I planned and had lots of options; some fell through, while others came to fruition."

Chief among the plans that fell through was the graduate program at Cambridge University's Classics department. A letter of rejection led Stephen to consider various service programs and law schools. Although he ultimately applied to law school, he thought it best to work for a community-building organization to further his work skills and strengthen his résumé. He applied to both AmeriCorps and City Year with hopes of working in New York for two years and studying for the LSAT. A couple of weeks after his interview with City Year, he was offered a position with the organization and is currently working with P.S. 344, an elementary school in East New York, Brooklyn.

Senior Year Regrets:

"I would have been a lot more proactive with regards to contacts and resources. I did everything myself and learned everything myself, which hurt me because I missed out on a lot of things I didn't know existed."

What College Taught Me:

"I learned that you cannot sit around waiting for the world to come to you. You have to put yourself out there if you want anything from life. I missed out on a lot during my college years because I was afraid and waited for things to come to me. If I was proactive, I could have gotten the full college experience. I also learned that you have to do what you love. You will be miserable if you get an economics degree just because you don't know what to do. If you like film studies, major in it and things will turn out well."

Life in the Real World:

"There is no process. There is no standard. School puts you into a mechanism, but the real world is just a jumble of systems. Put in the work and be proactive and you'll get yours. I get mine like Julius from the feature film *Remember the Titans*."

Advice for Graduates:

"Enjoy the last weeks of school and enjoy the summer if you go back home, because it might be your last true summer. If you don't have a job at the end of your senior year or aren't continuing your education, relax. You have so much time to figure it out; even if you don't know what you want to do with your life, just live it. You only get one. [There's no] sense wasting it on a Wall Street job that you absolutely hate. Money is nice, no way around it, but so are morality, community, and happiness. Use every single resource your school gives you and use every single contact you have available to try to find something. The more you put in, the more opportunities and choices you'll have after graduation."

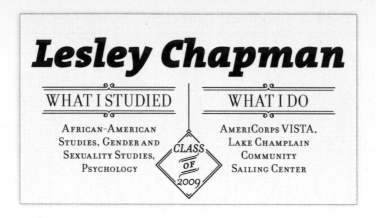

Lesley Chapman

WHAT I STUDIED

AFRICAN-AMERICAN STUDIES, GENDER AND SEXUALITY STUDIES, PSYCHOLOGY

CLASS OF 2009

WHAT I DO

AMERICORPS VISTA, LAKE CHAMPLAIN COMMUNITY SAILING CENTER

"I would say I was just sick of college."

Lesley welcomed graduation day with open arms. "I was pumped to do my own thing. I thought that college was a really overbearing place; you had to eat their food, live in their houses, etc. I was excited to have more independence. Just really over the whole college scene," she said. She had always contemplated a career in education, particularly library sciences, but was unsure if it was out of genuine interest or because her father was the principal at a K-12 school. She wanted to branch out and try working in a different setting to help find the right fit.

"I actually wound up using the career resource center at my school a lot. I tried to avoid talking too much to my dad about it and I found the jobs through my family, the career center at school, Craigslist, and online. I wound up going with the AmeriCorps position so that I could go out on my own and do my own thing for a while," she said.

About halfway through her first year with AmeriCorps, Lesley realized that education was the career for her and something she could do for the rest of her life. Disenchanted with her job and non-profits as a whole, she felt that it would be more effective and beneficial to work with kids as opposed to adults.

"I was surrounded by very well-intentioned adults who wanted to see a better world, but I found the non-profit world kind of toxic. Education seemed more sustainable and positive—I think that kids bring me a lot of joy and hope, whereas non-profits felt like we were trying to correct everything that was and is wrong with the world too late."

As a result, she decided to look for an assistant or substitute teacher position and will be enrolling in an M.A. program for Elementary and Early Childhood Education with the idea of becoming a teacher and/or librarian.

Senior Year Regrets:

"I wouldn't have accepted a job based on a phone interview! Never do that. I had a hideous sociopath as a boss, and didn't have any idea that was going to happen. She wasn't even on the phone during my interview!"

What College Taught Me:

"Oh man, a lot. For one, that I'm really good at reconstructing/ being angry/hating the world for all of its failings, but that that's not sustainable. It took me all of high school and most of college to learn that there's space for happiness in social justice, and that it's bullshit to spend your life being miserable so the world can be a better place. Doesn't work! Most of that wisdom is thanks to my mentor/professor/friend Gina Ulysse, who always encouraged me to find space for art and creativity! I learned that no matter how uncool it makes me, I need a minimum of eight hours of sleep, and that no matter what anyone tells you about their crazy workload, it's totally attainable."

Life in the Real World:

"Only work where you get respect. No matter how great the organization's mission is, if you're being treated like crap, it's not doing its job."

Advice for Graduates:

"Really, do what makes you happy. I learned a lot, mainly about dealing with psychopaths, but I should have quit and made lattes, my only real marketable skill leaving college. People keep saying, 'At least you learned a lot.' Yeah, I learned a lot while I was crying, not sleeping, ripping out my hair, and having my confidence destroyed, but nothing that I really wanted to learn. I guess the only real take-home lesson from that experience was that it's not worth it to spend fifty hours a week doing something that you hate. Don't get sucked into your school's ideas of what success entails, nor your friends'. Moving somewhere random and doing something random can be exactly what you need. And following your own passions is the most important thing, of course, but it can be damn hard to remember when everyone you know and love seems to be doing the same thing. It's a lot harder to explain a job in a field that no one has even heard of than to say, 'I'm doing the politically progressive thing that everyone else is doing.' But it can be rewarding and miserable and exactly what you need!"

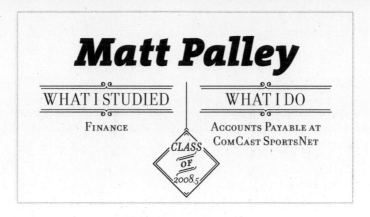

Matt Palley

WHAT I STUDIED

FINANCE

CLASS OF 2008.5

WHAT I DO

ACCOUNTS PAYABLE AT
COMCAST SPORTSNET

"Every day, I brainstormed about different things to do or different potential businesses to start."

Freshman year, Matt decided to take extra classes for the next six semesters, so he could graduate early and remain on campus for senior year. The strategy was to party often and spend time with friends without feeling overwhelmed by classes. "I was anxious to change the situation I was in," he said. "I wanted something new. While I now half-regret graduating college early, I needed to change my lifestyle of drinking every day, but had no plan or thoughts about what I wanted to do next." He knew he did not want to settle for the 9 to 5, but, unfortunately, that was his only option. After a few months of job searching following graduation, he was offered an unpaid internship with a sports TV channel. He believed that hard work as an intern would lead to a paid promotion.

Matt was keen on paying his dues, keeping his head down, and doing what he was told. After his internship, he was promoted to Front Office Coordinator, where he feels he can learn valuable skills and knowledge.

"My mindset at this point was not, 'I want to work hard for fifty years and attempt to climb the corporate ladder,'" he said. "I just wanted to earn my own living for a while and be in a position to continuously learn, so I could eventually use my growing skill set to start my own business. I wanted to start a sauce company and just come up with real good sauces, sweet, spicy, weird. Start setting up stands and see if it caught to the likings."

Senior Year Regrets:

"I would have applied for internships during sophomore and junior year summer breaks and tried to develop relationships within an industry that I wanted to get into."

What College Taught Me:

"I learned to make the most of the time I had there. Cherish it. Before you know it, you'll be forced to work."

Life in the Real World:

"I learned how easy it is to get discouraged. The 9-to-5 job can be extremely sluggish and stagnant compared to college life. It takes some getting used to."

Advice for Graduates:

"Don't spend hours online applying to Craigslist jobs that you wouldn't even want to do in the first place. Put a lot of extra effort into applying to jobs you truly may have interest in."

MY FIRST APARTMENT

"After graduating, I moved into the attic of my former college house to save money on rent. In order to get into my 'room,' you had to climb a very steep ladder. It was by far the grungiest place I have ever attempted to live in. After about a month of living up there, a terrible smell began to develop. Initially I shrugged it off, but it soon became unbearable. I decided that I needed to do some investigating. Under the futon I was sleeping on, I found a dead mouse that was quite far along in the decaying process. After cleaning it up, I realized mousetraps were a must. The next couple of weeks consisted of the mousetraps catching mice and the subsequent cleanup job. I'd rather have a real job and be living in a real room, but when the economy is in the tank, certain sacrifices are necessary."

Michael Yamashita

WHAT I STUDIED
ASIAN STUDIES

WHAT I DO
PHOTOGRAPHER

CLASS OF 1971

"I have never had a traditional interview. I would just take pictures and show them to people."

Michael's desire to learn about his own Asian culture and history originated from experiencing racism in high school. "I was dating a girl who had British parents that didn't want me to see her because I was Asian. That made me want to embrace my heritage and learn more about it in college," he said.

After spending his junior year abroad in London, he had thoughts of living abroad once he graduated, and often refers to his time in England as "a life changer." The excitement, change, and, as he puts it, "newness" of the experience left him with a desire for more. Combined with his interest in learning about Asian history and his culture, it is no surprise he wanted to travel and live abroad after college. "I was fed up with school," he said. "Coming back from London made that feeling even stronger. The draft was looming over everyone, and anxiety was just high on campus. I wanted those feelings I had in London again once I graduated."

When Michael graduated at the height of the Vietnam War, he had little to focus on outside of avoiding the draft. One of the doctors on campus agreed to fabricate a medical note stating he had gout, and thus was unable to serve in the military.

Through a family connection, Michael began working for an industrial marble company in Japan after receiving a one-way ticket to Tokyo as a graduation present. "My father worked for Mitsubishi and I was going to Japan for a job. I took some Japanese courses on the side, but the only thing I could really do was manual labor. I would unload trains that carried marble." Although he initially felt lonely because he was living in a dormitory-style building and was the only person whose native tongue was not Japanese, Michael began to embrace his new lifestyle after about a month. As he began to explore Japan, he wanted a way to share and capture his experiences other than writing letters back home or writing in a journal. An interest in photography was born.

"I never owned a camera or really took pictures before I was twenty-two," he said. "Initially, it was to show friends and family what I had done and places I've seen." What began as a hobby soon blossomed into an obsession. He would take pictures of anything and everything and always carried his camera with him. "As I took more and more pictures, I began to meet more and more people. I met some influential people who advised me and gave me some good advice." He slowly built up his portfolio while reaching out to different agencies. He hit it off with a small magazine in Tokyo called *Far East Traveler* and was hired for various projects. "You do a project, they like you, they have you do another and that leads to something else," he said.

Senior Year Regrets:

"If I had the time and money, I would have gotten into photography earlier. I would have done it more senior year, but I had surgery on both of my ankles and was on crutches for the entire year. I also wish I studied languages more."

What College Taught Me:

"College made me a more rounded person, gave me skills to do my own studies, taught me how to think and stand up on my own, and gave me a certain confidence to see what is out there in the world."

Life in the Real World:

"I have been using connections from school in my professional life. As a student, I was not prepared for the real world at all. College gave me confidence and a foundation to get out there."

Advice for Graduates:

"This has always been a one percent of one percent business. It's very popular and open. Anyone can do it, regardless of degrees. Even with a degree, it doesn't guarantee a place in the industry. It's your passion that will drive you and tell you whether or not it's right for you. You really gotta believe in yourself."

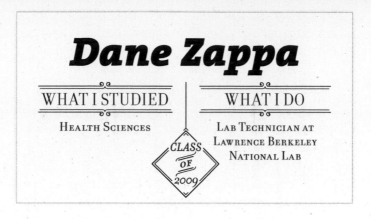

Dane Zappa

WHAT I STUDIED

HEALTH SCIENCES

WHAT I DO

LAB TECHNICIAN AT
LAWRENCE BERKELEY
NATIONAL LAB

CLASS
OF
2009

"The real world is always changing, so when I see people who are able to roll will the punches, do what they love, and become successful individuals out of it, I try to model myself after them."

With his senior year ending in early December, Dane used the winter months to intensely study and prepare for the MCAT exams he would take in January. "School isn't ending for me for a very long time, and I'm definitely anxious about the next step," he said. "In my freshman year it was, 'Don't wake me until 2:00 p.m.' and in my senior year it was, 'Don't bother me while I'm studying.'" He made sure to keep his options very open and applied for various laboratory and medical positions in the event he didn't get into medical school, but also with the intention of giving himself some work experience. Unfortunately, he wasn't admitted to any of the schools he applied to, which made him truly understand how hard the process is on a personal level.

"It's easy for someone to tell you how difficult the [medical school] process is, but I definitely didn't understand that until I went through it. Not getting in made me think about other options, but only options that are related to the healthcare field.

I think, if anything, rejection from medical school strengthened my resolve not necessarily to go to medical school, but to stay in health care and do what I could to help people," he said.

Looking to strengthen his application for the following year, as well as earn money and gain work experience, Dane took a job as a lab technician that has proven to be informative and helpful, both personally and professionally.

"All medical schools are looking for laboratory experience, because so much of understanding immunology and microbiology can really only be studied in a lab...Working in a lab in a field other than biology gives me a good diverse research background while still showing that I have experience working in a lab." Now that he has been through the process and understands the intricacies, Dane is enjoying the experience he has gained in the industry as he bolsters what he hopes will be an acceptable résumé and medical school application.

Senior Year Regrets:
"Start looking for work sooner, like during the actual term."

What College Taught Me:
"To answer this would take a small novel, and would probably be filled with really corny quotes, because that really is what college is like. Or, you could watch all of those ridiculous college movies (*Animal House*, *Van Wilder*, etc.) and get a pretty good idea of the values of college."

Life in the Real World:
"I think the most successful people in the real world—with

careers, relationships both social and romantic, health, etc.—especially those in the 22-25 age group, and not that I consider myself super successful, [have] the ability to go with the flow. Humans have this uncanny tendency to want to grow up at an earlier and earlier age. What this means is we end up restricting ourselves with niches and roles, such as taking middle school too seriously in preparation for that one career path we'll be on for the next forty-five years, and so if things don't work out, or work out differently, there is a feeling of failure or that we don't measure up. The real world is always changing, so when I see people who are able to roll will the punches, do what they love, and become successful individuals out of it, I try to model myself after them."

Advice for Graduates:

"It's, unfortunately, not so much about your résumé as it is about who you know, especially with a bachelor's degree. I believe using family and friends is the best way to find work, especially if you don't mind doing stuff like waiting tables for a while."

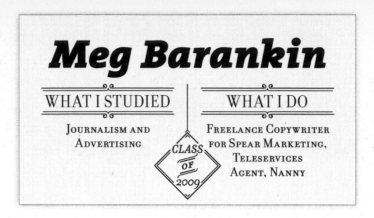

Meg Barankin

WHAT I STUDIED

Journalism and Advertising

CLASS OF 2009

WHAT I DO

Freelance Copywriter for Spear Marketing, Teleservices Agent, Nanny

"For most of senior year, I kind of had a 'figure it out later' mindset."

Meg's interests and skill level led her to think a career in public relations would suit her best after graduation. However, as college progressed, she began to excel in her advertising classes and contemplate exactly how she would use her skills to obtain a job. "I was pretty focused on doing well in my advertising classes so that I would build the portfolio to be able to eventually get the job I wanted, and just learning about the profession in general, but I didn't know what to do with my writing background," she said.

For Meg, the most important thing during senior year was to spend time with friends by going to parties and taking trips off campus. Graduation arrived without a job offer, and although she was sad about school ending, she was excited by the idea of moving to a new city to find work.

"I found all of my jobs on Craigslist once I moved. The hardest part was leaving for Portland [Oregon] after going back to my parents' house after graduation; that home had always been my *home* that I would come back to after a year of school, or during breaks, and realizing that that wasn't the case anymore was hard, and a little scary."

Senior Year Regrets:

"I would have used the career center more, and tried to get more help with contacts in the journalism department. I really just relied on the Internet, rather than people I knew."

What College Taught Me:

"Managing my time with friends. A lot of times I'll make plans with multiple people and overextend myself and end up flaking on somebody, and I really don't like this about myself. I also learned that I'm a smart person. It's not that I thought I *wasn't* smart before, but in high school I was surrounded by overachievers, and I never really considered myself an academic person. I discovered that when I took classes that were really interesting to me, and when the content was inspiring and motivating, I became a straight-A student. That felt good."

Life in the Real World:

"It's not easy, and the important thing is to keep persevering. There are times when you think you'll never find a job, things will never get better, and you might as well just give up. You can't let yourself do that. Also, as cheesy as it may sound, I've learned that the phrase 'everything happens for a reason' is pretty true."

Advice for Graduates:

"Don't give up. It's really easy to get discouraged/depressed when you're trying to find a job. Because of how hard it is for everyone right now, don't feel like you *need* to get a job that will lead to the career you want. Take a restaurant or café job. Make sure you're making some money and getting some sort of job experience, and then focus on doing what you need to do to get your career going. There's nothing wrong with getting hired by an incredible company straight out of college, but there's also nothing wrong, and this is more likely, with working menial jobs and enjoying your life while you build career skills and figure things out. If that's where you're at, do not feel bad about it. Use the resources you have at your college, and enjoy your last year. Don't let yourself get too stressed out about finding a job and let it ruin your last year with your friends."

John Griffin

WHAT I STUDIED

ENGLISH AND
AMERICAN STUDIES

CLASS
OF
1970

WHAT I DO

VICE PRESIDENT OF
PUBLISHING AT
*National
Geographic*
(RETIRED)

"I was only thinking about two things going into my senior year: the Vietnam War and women."

Even though he was a student at an all-male college, John never considered it a problem until his junior year, at which point he decided to transfer and spend the first semester of his senior year at Vassar College. With his attention focused only on women and avoiding the draft, he had no post-graduation plans. "Nobody was really thinking of anything but the war," he said. "I was part of some demonstrations and protests. It was a really anxious time for everyone." He knew he would avoid the draft as a conscientous objector and contemplated different industries in which he would want to pursue a career. "I always wanted to go into publishing. I was into the editorial side of it. I grew up in a house full of magazines and newspapers, and my family was into current events, so I was always thinking about it."

In order to justify his draft status, John needed to get a service job immediately. He turned to the classifieds section of the *Boston Herald* and was hired to make beds in a hospital. "It was training for a total of four hours. One hour was spent on general anatomy and three hours on bed-making." He quit after one week. Despite his limited experience in a hospital atmosphere, he was quickly hired as an aide in a psychiatric hospital, where he worked the graveyard shift. "I made sure nobody ran out of the building," he said. "I watched people on suicide watch. I learned the difference between being crazy and being sane is not what you feel or perceive, but rather how you take things in, accept them, and react to them."

John then decided he wanted to go into education, so he quit his job at the psychiatric hospital and was hired as an assistant teacher to children with attention deficit disorder. "I got the job through a teammate of mine from a recreational basketball league," he said. "But I didn't have the patience to work in that field and figured that out a few months in." He then moved to Martha's Vineyard, where a friend of his from college got him a job at a leather shop selling belts and shoes.

John realized that if he wanted to work in publishing, he should actually give it a try. So he moved to New York, visiting employment agencies in person in pursuit of a job. He was, to his surprise, hired by a small publishing house on the Upper West Side a few weeks after moving to the city. "It was this small hippie company on West 78th and Broadway," he said. "They focused on education materials. I had a beard, was anti-war, and overall [was] a little unkempt, and they liked it." After three months, however, he was put in charge of the entire publishing firm following the resignation of his boss.

"I was responsible for seven social science readers and once they were completed, 350,000 copies had spelling errors and we sent them to prisons. I worked the last three months for no money before the company went bankrupt. Then I traveled." He ventured across country—kayaking, backpacking, and staying in youth hostels—and wound up in Anchorage, Alaska, where he got a job as a restaurant dishwasher.

With his desire to continue his travels remaining steadfast, John and his wife went to Africa, where they travelled through remote areas of Kenya and what was then Southern Sudan in two Land Rovers with eight other travelers.

"The cars were breaking down constantly. One time we hitched a ride on a well drilling truck and sat with goats, chickens, and other hitchhikers. It was a blast. When I returned to the United States, I thought I would become a freelance writer, and an old friend told me Rodale Press was hiring a managing/circulation manager for their *Exceptional Parent* magazine, and even though I had no idea why they hired me, they did."

Senior Year Regrets:

"I do wish I worked harder in college. I should have been involved with the school paper since I wanted to go into publishing. I wish I had been more serious about studies."

What College Taught Me:

"I learned the world is full of talented people and there is so much to learn. I learned that I could succeed in an intense, high-powered environment. I learned how to really write. I also learned about the explosion of drugs, as it was the '60s and all."

Life in the Real World:

"I was really lucky and stupid, especially with my first job in New

York. I learned you have to be open to things. I had confidence that came from my mom and to do what you love and it will all work out. I wanted to work in publishing and I wanted to travel and see the world. My dad kept saying that I was crazy."

Advice for Graduates:

"I always say the same thing: follow your nose. Do what you love. Try to get a job with it. You have no idea where life is going to take you. Trust your instincts. Be a humanities major. Expand your mind. That's what helps you deal with the world. Read great literature. Try to be positive. Never settle. If it's not right for you, move on. The key to success is effort over time. You can't be jumping around. You have to know ultimately where you want to go. Whatever your job is, how does what you do fit into the big picture. What is your purpose? [You should be] constantly looking up and out, not down."

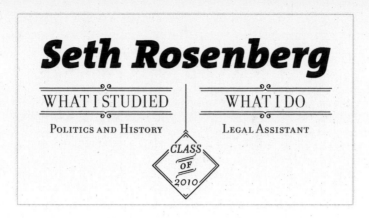

Seth Rosenberg

WHAT I STUDIED
Politics and History

WHAT I DO
Legal Assistant

CLASS OF 2010

"Life is good!"

Enrolled as a part-time student and living with friends in an apartment off campus, Seth was the most comfortable and relaxed he had been at any point during college. "I had developed very strong friendships over the past three years and also had three years of experience under my belt, which made me very familiar with the atmosphere, culture, and people. Being a senior, I wanted to make the most of my experience," he said. Spending the majority of his time with the friends he had made was easily the highlight of senior year for Seth, and when his last semester started he could only think, "What the heck am I going to do afterwards?!"

Although he had ambitions of becoming a music producer and/or farmer, Seth turned his attention to law, knowing there were usually entry-level positions open to recent college graduates. He researched the companies and organizations he planned on contacting, and also decided to speak with his parents about what types of questions he might encounter. "Over the past couple of years, I have found that over-preparation, if [that's] even possible, is always better than under-preparation. Practice is always helpful."

Senior Year Regrets:

"An earlier start on reaching out to potential employers, perhaps. Informational interviews, even over the phone if possible. I felt pretty good about the effort I made, considering I was far away from the location I wanted to live [in]."

What College Taught Me:

"I experienced a lot of personal growth throughout my time at college. Freshman year was an exciting time to meet people and live away from my parents for the first time, surrounded by my peers. Over the four years, and particularly because I was in a small school in a small town, I was able to get a new understanding of my own personality and develop my own individuality in a way that never really happened before. I think a lot of this can be attributed to the relative isolation I experienced in college compared to growing up in a populated urban place. The social scene at Oberlin was very much centered on and around campus and required some strong friendships and creativity to keep ourselves entertained. The winter term program at school helped me learn about potential career paths and get some (limited) work experience. Not only was I able to do several internships at nonprofits in Oakland, California, but I also was able to work on an organic farm in Hawaii one winter, which opened my eyes to a different lifestyle and sparked an interest in sustainable agriculture. Being in Ohio, I learned what real season changes are.

My senior year, I learned what it was like to rent an apartment and pay my own bills through part-time work."

Life in the Real World:

"Living in the real world has been a really positive experience for me after graduating from college, but that is not to say it hasn't had its challenges. There are more freedoms, but more responsibilities. There are different kinds of opportunities, but they are generally more competitive. The job search can be really discouraging, and social life can be less stimulating without being immediately surrounded by so many people of the same age. But I find participating in the real world to be just that: more 'real' than the college world. I feel like I am getting a step closer to making my dreams come true."

Advice for Graduates:

"First of all, don't stress. Secondly, pursue what you really want to do, not what you think you should do or what you imagine will make the most money. If you don't know what you want to do, try something you think you might enjoy. The only way to truly find out is by doing; you probably have more options than it may seem. Don't be scared to make phone calls, send e-mails, pursue independent projects, or even travel if you have the resources. You are young and you have the rest of your life to go to Plan B. This is the time where you can afford to take risks and fail and learn about yourself. Also, try to foster the relationships with people who you look up to or respect at school—teachers, alumni, peers—because they might be the key to opening the door to opportunities."

Arian Gower

WHAT I STUDIED

BIOCHEMISTRY

CLASS OF 2009

WHAT I DO

GRADUATE STUDENT
AT CHICAGO MEDICAL
SCHOOL

"Twenty-three years old and still dreaming."

For Arian, senior year was about putting himself in the best position for medical school, while also spending as much time with friends as possible. Admittedly, he didn't plan things out as well as he liked; he took a year off after graduating with nothing in mind besides living at home and studying for the MCAT. "I was pretty confused and anxious upon graduating. Living at home with nothing to do is really only cool for the first few weeks," he said.

Arian decided to hedge his bets and applied to a master's program in biomedical science in case he did not get into medical school. This approach proved fruitful, as he was admitted only to graduate school. "It doesn't help that I'm from California, where the medical schools are nearly impossible to get into. The plan is to power through the master's program. If all goes well, I will use my master's degree to strengthen my application for medical school."

Senior Year Regrets:

"This is tricky. I had a job lined up in Boston, but my salary would have been insufficient to finish the year with a profit. I decided to head home and try my luck. I will never really know if I made the right decision. The recession didn't help."

What College Taught Me:

"Grades matter, friendships count, and every experience, good or bad, is a growing experience. If you live far from your college, keep in touch with friends because each one represents a place to crash when you decide to go back and visit."

Life in the Real World:

"Real life is no joke. It's harder than it was for LeBron James to win a championship. Now, if you have good connections and friends, you may find yourself in a position to get an interview, but nothing is guaranteed. It's sad to say, but I found most job opportunities on Craigslist. I submitted over sixty-five applications and heard back from only six. It's tough out there."

Advice for Graduates:

"Start early and make connections. It's easier if you're looking for a job around your school. It's tough, unless you directly know someone, to find a job outside of your school's state; in my case, it was a separate coast. Student loans are no joke. Find a job or expect to continue your education. Sure, take a year off, travel, do what you need to do, but nothing sucks more than not knowing what the next step is in your life. The faster you find that, the less anxious you and your parents will be."

Adrian Ma

WHAT I STUDIED

AEROSPACE ENGINEERING

CLASS OF 2009

WHAT I DO

SYSTEMS ENGINEER FOR
UNITED STATES NAVY

"I wholeheartedly agree with the saying that college is some of the best years of your life."

If money weren't an issue, Adrian would love to become a kindergarten or first grade teacher, even though he has devoted more than four years to engineering. "A friend's mother, who was a K-1 teacher herself, told me to make money first, then become a teacher," he said. His ultimate dream scenario, however, would be to travel, eat, and document it, like Anthony Bourdain or Andrew Zimmern. Since he lacked a culinary history and writing background, Adrian turned his attention to jobs for which he was better suited. He attended several job fairs without much success; each company was looking for someone with experience and, as a senior in college, he had none. "I was very apprehensive about working eight-hour days in a cubicle doing engineering, and I figured that if I didn't get a job by summer, I'd look into either the military or going to graduate school."

Out of the many booths at the job fairs Adrian went to, the one where the interest was mutual was with the United States Navy. After submitting his résumé online, he learned that the Navy was quite eager to hire recent graduates, and it extended an offer to him two months after he interviewed. "I tried to embellish my school work on my résumé without telling an outright lie, and worked on presenting myself as well as possible. I also invested in getting a suit for in-person interviews."

Adrian works in the Torpedo Systems Department at the Naval Undersea Warfare Center, where he is responsible for various aspects related to torpedoes. including: prototypes and demos of new technologies; transitioning new technologies into existing/new torpedoes; testing these technologies in the field (on submarines, ships, and aircraft); and ensuring the functionality of existing weapons that are being used by the American fleet.

"The first few weeks were a mixture of excitement, overwhelming information, and boredom," he said. "As a new hire, I tried to present myself as a blank slate, open to learning how everything worked since my work was still being defined and I hadn't been put on a project yet. All in all, it was pretty interesting."

Senior Year Regrets:
"I would have sent out even more applications than I already did in order to widen my chances."

What College Taught Me:
"To get by in college and life, you don't necessarily need to be the best, just better than average. It's important to balance fun and work, which can be difficult, but it is possible."

Life in the Real World:
"Like college, looking for a job and the 'real world' are what you

make out of them. Things are a little tougher and you now have more things to worry about, but it's not as big a transition as you might fear. I've learned, at least at my job, that they don't expect you to know everything right off the bat, and it's important to show a willingness to learn."

Advice for Graduates:

"Start early with looking for internships and doing work in school related to your major. Utilize all available resources: career centers, faculty, friends, family, job websites, etc. In a tough economy, beggars can't be choosers; if you can find a job, it's better in the long run to get an unpaid internship related to your major than to get paid working at a mall or as a waiter. While it may be easier to find and apply for local jobs, don't limit yourself by searching only locally.

"I would advise you to submit as many applications to different companies as possible; don't just focus on one job. If you can't find a job or are still searching, consider an internship or volunteering for something in the line of work that you are interested in to at least get some experience. Another option would be to consider going back to school and getting a graduate degree."

Mark Debuque

WHAT I STUDIED	WHAT I DO
COMMUNICATIONS AND JOURNALISM	HOTEL CONCIERGE

CLASS OF 2008

"Living paycheck to paycheck on Avenue C."

Mark believes that any job unrelated to music is simply a means to an end and will consider employment that gives him flexibility to focus on his true passion. "I truly am only aspiring to make a living off of recording, performing, and producing music," he said. "Anything else will serve as taking care of what I have to [do] to get by."

Even though he had been a fan of hip hop since elementary school and was part of a rap group in college called Central Intelligence, Mark did not major in music because he was not interested in composition nor the study of music. "Strangely enough, I am not very musically inclined at all. I just have a good ear for what I like and a sense of internal rhythm. Songwriting to me is more the manifestation of literature to music than the actual study of music itself."

As graduation approached, he was experiencing a variety of emotions ranging from nostalgia to worry to excitement. Chief among those feelings, however, was relief that he wouldn't have to sit through a class he cared little about and could devote his time to pursuing music.

"Freshman year, I cared nothing about a real job. I would party and meet girls as much as possible, and graduation seemed like it was a decade away. Senior year, I was definitely much more mature, but I still didn't know exactly what I would be doing in the field I had chosen. I also was looking forward to getting the degree because I realized long before that I was in a major that I cared little about and it was a matter of getting it done and moving on," he said.

Mark figured that living in New York would be best for his music career, so he moved after graduation with enough money for two months' worth of rent while scouring Craigslist for employment opportunities. "The first interview I got was with the hotel I work for now, which I heard about on Craigslist. I practiced basic [interview] answers. I tried to make my responses as eloquent and smooth as possible. I have always been good off the cuff, so I actually didn't prepare a whole lot," he said.

Senior Year Regrets:

"I regret not approaching the business end of music in school. I feel like in hindsight that could have really benefited me now that I know what it takes. I would have spent much more time preparing a résumé and looking into the move to New York more than I did. I didn't bring much money with me other than [for] two months rent. I would have sought out more advice and certainly could have benefited from some sort of handbook."

What College Taught Me:

"College isn't necessarily for everyone. You get out what you put in, as is anything in life. If I could do it over, I wouldn't have gone. But it was ingrained in my mind that you need college to succeed in life. Being an artist, I've taught myself and learned from situations that didn't lend themselves to classrooms. But I guess that growth period was necessary, as I learned how to grow up during that point."

Life in the Real World:

"The 'real' world is probably a bit different than I expected. Rent day doesn't change, and Con Edison and light bills don't seem to recognize your potential as an artist, but rather they need money to stay on. Establishing a good rapport with your place of employment is pretty important, I've found. You can't burn bridges as you may done as an exuberant youth. You're an adult now. Things matter more. Professional relationships, whichever avenue you choose to go down, will help set you up for your chosen future."

Advice for Graduates:

"Follow [your] dreams to the end of the earth, but make a very solid contingency plan. Make sure your contingency plan has a backup contingency plan. It is important to take risks in life and it really is the only way to get ahead, but planning for these risks in case things go awry is what makes the success rate of a plan much higher. Seek advice, research your future, and dream and think big."

Daniel Handler

WHAT I STUDIED

ENGLISH AND
AMERICAN STUDIES

CLASS OF 1992

WHAT I DO

AUTHOR ALSO
KNOWN AS
LEMONY SNICKET,
ACCORDIONIST

"As my position post-graduation involved staying at school, I was mostly anxious about looking like a loser hanging around school after graduation."

Daniel had known he wanted to be a writer since he had been a small boy. As he started his senior year in college, he began researching and applying to scholarships and fellowships that would allow him to pursue his interest in writing. Early in his senior year, he was given a fellowship that was awarded annually to a student pursuing independent research and/or creative writing. The award included free housing for the year, as well as a small living stipend. As a result, he wasn't worried about what he would do immediately after graduation, and was free to focus on his undergraduate thesis and his friends.

In return for the free housing, however, he had to participate in various events on campus at which he was required to be a server and bartender. "This [the fellowship] seemed like a great way to hole up for a year and write and find out if I was actually suited for the sort of isolation required from a novelist. I was and I am," he said.

"My situation is somewhat unusual, as I wanted to be a novelist, which is not a position for which one can interview. I held a series of jobs that I chose based on the amount of free time they'd leave me to work on a book. For example, I was a dance class pianist, a laundry assistant, a bartender, and an administrative assistant."

Senior Year Regrets:
"Nothing."

What College Taught Me:
"Good people will nourish you forever. Bad people will fuck you up. Read a lot. Get enough sleep. Try to be as kind as you can to everyone."

Life in the Real World:
"There is no 'real world.' There is only this one. Everyone in it is nervous and scared a good deal of the time, so much of what they say is going to be nonsense. Forgive the nonsense, but don't believe it."

Advice for Graduates:
"Don't move anyplace where you don't have a support network. Spend time with friends, but don't drink or sleep around too much. Don't imagine for a moment that everyone else isn't as confused as you are. Great people at the workplace, trustworthy people with integrity who are doing good work, are more important than the job itself. Snatch any opportunity to be near people doing good, inspiring work, and quit lousy situations as soon as you can."

RUNNING INTO AN OLD CLASSMATE

"One day, maybe a year after graduating, I was cranky over the fact that I didn't seem to be getting closer to doing what I wanted to do. I called some friends and we had drinks and went to the movies, but it wasn't helping. I left the movie theater and walked out into the rain and bought a bottle of water and stood outside drinking it and feeling miserable. A taxi pulled up and out came a guy I knew in high school. I'd never liked him. He was dressed up and looked healthy and happy. He asked me what I was up to and I said, 'Nothing.' He told me that everything in his life was going wonderfully and he was doing some terrible, boring thing for a living and making loads of money. He walked away smirking and I vowed I would never again spend time envying people I didn't admire."

The
No-Ideas

THOSE WHO DIDN'T KNOW
WHAT THEY WANTED TO DO
ONCE THEY GRADUATED.

Sean Collins

WHAT I STUDIED	WHAT I DO
AMERICAN STUDIES	MATH TEACHER

CLASS OF 2008

"It was either General Manager for the Boston Celtics or Catherine Zeta-Jones's trophy husband."

Before senior year, Sean didn't know what he wanted to do after college. He found himself shooting down various career opportunities that either he thought of or were suggested to him by friends and family.

"I have the type of personality where I would always find some reason why I thought I wouldn't like a particular job," he said. "I probably researched almost everything, e.g., financial advisor, firefighter, FBI agent, architect, engineer, actuary, college coach, and psychologist, unless I knew for sure that I was against it. For example, I knew I didn't want to be a lawyer, an accountant, or a doctor."

Sean realized he had to be flexible, so he took a leap of faith by enrolling in a teaching and counseling program at the suggestion of a friend from college.

"I was always a person trying to find the perfect career," he said. "It meant a lot to me to find an enjoyable career and to do something I could be proud of. During senior year, I was frantically searching through careers and trying to decide what I wanted to do with my life. I loved college, but honestly, I was pretty sick of going to the same parties and all of the work. I was pretty excited to do something new."

Filtering through his likes and dislikes for potential work environments aided Sean in his job search and also provided some insight into his own character. "I like the social atmosphere of schools, and I was pretty opposed to sitting in a cubicle all day with no interaction. Also, I think some of it came down to analyzing my strengths and weaknesses. I knew that I wouldn't be any good at jobs that required salesmanship or monotonous research. Schools were just a very familiar environment that I had a positive association with," he said. After a six-week training course with the New Teacher's Project the summer after graduating, he was placed in a middle school in Memphis, Tennessee, as a math teacher and basketball coach.

Senior Year Regrets:

"I think I might have looked into school counseling sooner; I wanted to apply to a program, but it was too late by the time that I came to that realization. With that said, I am glad that I spent a year teaching and decided to pursue it. It was an invaluable life experience."

What College Taught Me:

"One of the biggest things I learned in college was how to act in different social situations."

Life in the Real World:

"I learned how to be assertive [by] working as a teacher and a coach. It was a 'sink-or-swim' job, and I needed to learn that skill pretty quickly. It was very weird going from that egalitarian, laid-back environment of college to being an authority figure. Honestly, the first year of working probably changed my personality more than four years of college. At first, it was just an act, but if you act enough, it becomes a skill."

Advice for Graduates:

"I would suggest talking to people who do that stuff for a living, such as a career counselor. You might not find the perfect fit, but you can probably avoid choosing a career that is totally wrong for you. Talk to people in those fields that you are interested in. Don't stress too much. Use all available resources, and network."

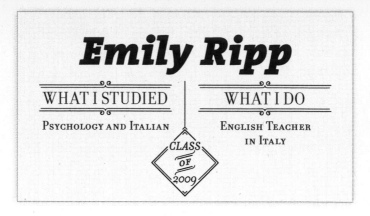

"I felt that college trapped me in this pre-adult limbo, where I was supported and coddled, and then [I was] thrown out into the adult world without any guidance on how to survive."

When Emily started college, she thought she would study theater or psychology, even though she didn't know the first thing about psychology. "I declared a major in psychology after taking one psych course because I was on a deadline to make a decision and my major advisor gave me her signature," she said. By junior year, she began to think about her life after school and considered childhood education or occupational therapy. "I found myself drawn to the chapters in my textbook on early childhood development and education. All of my internships and fieldwork opportunities throughout college were focused on alternative assessment, developmental disabilities, and early intervention for children with disabilities," she said. As a senior, however, she became dissatisfied with the path she had been taking and wanted to try something different.

"I found the professional environments to be rather stagnant, socially. A lot of single and middle-aged women. The daily work consisted of a lot of BS and bureaucracy, such as analyzing children's progress, applying psychological theories inappropriately, and labeling conditions that seemed more to appease the source of public funding than assist the child in any way. I refused to settle on a career by default, and I'm still deciding what that something different could possibly be."

For Emily, the feelings that came with graduation were very conflicting. "I was happy to leave college, as the four years of living in a bubble were getting to feel a bit claustrophobic. That said, as soon as I left college I missed the ease of having my entire social life concentrated on one campus. I was eager to work, to work toward a professional reputation and a paycheck rather than a grade in a teacher's book."

The only thing she wanted to do once she graduated was return to Italy, where she had studied abroad for a semester in her junior year. "I refused to apply to graduate school right out of college, as I was undecided about my next step and did not consider grad school a viable backup plan," she said. "Grad school is a specialization, an investment in a career path, and I was not about to pick a program out of a hat." She decided her best route back to Italy would be through teaching English in some capacity, so she applied to a teaching certification program with the idea that she could find a job once she was actually in Italy; she was accepted.

Senior Year Regrets:
"I would have lined up backup plans like my mother told me to. Ugh."

What College Taught Me:

"Your friendships and social memories stay with you much longer than the dates for that art history final. I came out of college feeling like I honed a great deal of general skills: critical thinking, analytical writing, fact memorization, working under pressure... I just need to learn how to apply them in a non-school setting, which is something I was not taught in school."

Life in the Real World:

"Everyone around you loves to give advice; apply your situation to their own, whether past or present; and nudge their way into your mental process. My instinctive reaction to being lectured and advised is to let the speaker run their mouth and feign interest while asserting that his or her situation is nowhere near comparable to my own. Recently, that defense mechanism has crawled into a hole and festered, because the truth is, everyone has something valuable to offer."

Advice for Graduates:

"Don't get disheartened and don't take it personally if you don't get a job. Whether the economy is booming or in a recession, there are always going to be competitors to the nth degree vying for the same positions as you, and you could get taken out of the running because of a typo in your subject line or an applicant whose daddy knows the boss. And don't be afraid to sell yourself. It's so uncomfortable and awkward to brag about your 'skills' in an e-mail, but if you don't have confidence in your abilities, why should a recruiter? Network the old-fashioned way. Rather than tweet or twit or twat or whatnot, go shake somebody's hand and make eye contact...meet people! Don't rely on your cyber profiles to make a good impression for you. I researched language schools to become certified as a teacher of English as a second language. And then I researched language schools in Italy once I was certified. I mentally prepared mini-demo lessons in case I was asked to mock teach the interviewer, which I had been told happens when looking for teaching work. I found out about opportunities through websites, mostly, and word of mouth through friends and parents."

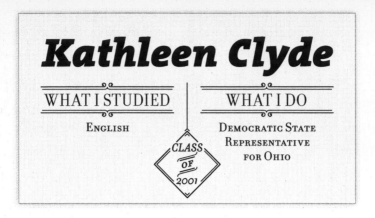

Kathleen Clyde

WHAT I STUDIED

ENGLISH

CLASS OF 2001

WHAT I DO

DEMOCRATIC STATE
REPRESENTATIVE
FOR OHIO

"Honestly, I did not know what I wanted to do when I graduated."

Freshman year often evokes various feelings and opinions: some love starting college, others hate it, and some are just lost. "I didn't really know what I was doing as a freshman," Kathleen said. "I was not prepared." Looking for some stability and structure, she decided to try out for the track team. Once she made the team and became more acclimated to college, she began to enjoy herself.

When Kathleen graduated, she was certain only that she was going to travel through Europe for six weeks and then move back to her hometown of Garrettsville, Ohio. Once home, she had no clue where she wanted to take her life, so she drove across the country visiting friends and enjoying her summer. After the road trip, she reached out to Community Shelter Board, a non-profit that she had interned with the summer before her senior year. "The Executive Director was a close family friend, and my dad made the initial contact before I got the internship; they hired me full time once I graduated after I submitted my résumé."

After only a few months on the job, she applied to law school, but, unfortunately, did not get in. "Funding for my non-profit, or, specifically, my position, began to run out, so I looked into other options."

Making the choice to move away from home and try something new, she moved to Jersey City, New Jersey, to live with her brother and give the fashion industry a try in New York. "I don't really know what I wanted to do in fashion. I ended up as an intern in a corporate showroom for a small designer," she said. Kathleen had a part-time waitressing gig to complement the fashion internship, but both industries began to wear on her. She moved back to Ohio and set her sights on politics.

"My internship wrapped up in the summer of 2004, which was just when the Bush vs. Kerry election was heating up and Ohio was the center of everything. I remember thinking to myself that I had to get back to my home state and try to help get Kerry elected. I would be more useful there doing that than I was in New York City in the fashion industry. I got the statewide student coordinator job for the Kerry campaign by volunteering full time (unpaid) for a week, and then applying for it. Throughout this whole time, I applied to law school again and was accepted, but deferred a year to finish working on the campaign."

Senior Year Regrets:
"Gotten involved with politics earlier. Maybe joined a campus group."

What College Taught Me:

"The interpersonal relationships with all sorts of people. I got an overall quality education with a sense of giving back. That mission stayed with me. There are different walks of life, and meeting people from different parts of the country and world was so unique."

Life in the Real World:

"Work really carefully to craft a good reputation. Always be willing to do what is needed. Work hard. Help out. It's a lot about building connections. Keeping care. Never applied to a job 'cold.'"

Advice for Graduates:

"Hang in there. Find something you are passionate about and go after it. There are lots of folks out there who want to help you. Be positive and energetic. Get involved in politics. We need people in politics."

MY FIRST APARTMENT

"When I lived with my brother in Jersey City, I was in a room where I couldn't stand up without hitting my head on the ceiling. It was about the size of a closet."

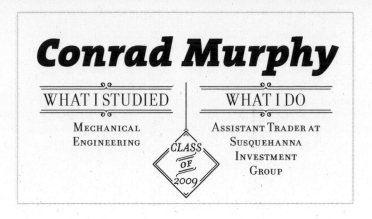

Conrad Murphy

WHAT I STUDIED

MECHANICAL
ENGINEERING

CLASS OF 2009

WHAT I DO

ASSISTANT TRADER AT
SUSQUEHANNA
INVESTMENT
GROUP

"The last time we do [insert activity here] took over my life, with the blank representing a college-only activity that could never be duplicated."

It wasn't until his senior year that Conrad ended up finding subjects he liked studying: engineering and robotics. He was unsure how to translate his interests in specific classes into a job, however, so he began to apply to banking and management positions because there were more companies in those fields. "Although I was really good at robotics, I looked around and didn't see a whole lot of robotics companies out there," he said. "Although my skills were useful for a lot of other engineering jobs, I had a difficult time getting excited for those jobs."

Accepting the idea of graduating and entering the work force was a two-year process for Conrad. In the fall of his senior year, he was looking to apply to engineering positions while also applying to a graduate program at the same institution he was enrolled with as an undergraduate. "I spent a lot of time right after I got to school during senior year working on my job situation. Engineering companies didn't want to hire young engineers, since we take a lot of job-specific training before we produce useful work." Conrad elected to go to graduate school with the idea of boosting his credentials and skill set while also hoping the job market would be better later down the road.

Although he wanted a clean tech job in Silicon Valley, Conrad thought he should cast a wider net and, therefore, decided to interview for several very different positions. After a few interviews with various companies, he was hired as a trader for a company he had never heard of in a city, Philadelphia, he had never been to. "None of my interviews went that well, but the numbers are never in your favor when they interview eighty people for three jobs. Every interview I had was arranged through the online job board at my school, except for one from an e-mail list for my grad program and one from a résumé my brother passed on to his employer."

Senior Year Regrets:
"I would have been a little more proactive [in] reaching out to my network of friends and family for a job."

What College Taught Me:
"I learned what makes me happy. I also learned that it comes down to intangibles. When you are more than a résumé and a number, I feel like there is less luck involved."

Life in the Real World:
"What you do is not who you are. Especially now, while you're young in the new economy, there is nothing wrong with changing jobs, going back to grad school, or being a ski instructor/camp counselor/financial drain on your parents. Well, clearly that last

one is not a good idea, and graduating without debt, I admit I'm looking at this from a privileged perspective, but right now I'm in a job that I'm not sure is a great fit for me, and I'm okay with that.

"Two years ago the idea of being in the 'wrong job' scared me more than being in the 'wrong school' did five years ago. Especially right out of college, with no family responsibilities and the ability to live on ramen for weeks at a time, the idea of 'following the path' exactly doesn't scare me. Now, if this job doesn't work out or I get fired in six months, I'm okay with that, and the feeling will probably be mutual. I will find a situation that works for me."

Advice for Graduates:

"During an internship, you should certainly be thinking about a full-time job with the company. You should have this conversation before you leave, [if] for no other reason [than] you will know where you stand. Job hunting is a numbers game. The shotgun approach can backfire if you don't put effort [into] applications and it shows, but it is critical to have a lot of lottery tickets, especially in this economy where companies can get a hundred applications per opening. That means only one percent of applications are successful, and ninety-nine percent of you are not getting the job. That was difficult for me at first, since I wasn't used to not succeeding. It isn't really like school where you can study hard and get an A, since you are competing against everyone else who applies. You might not be the best applicant, there is nothing you can do about that, and the best thing to do is find another opening."

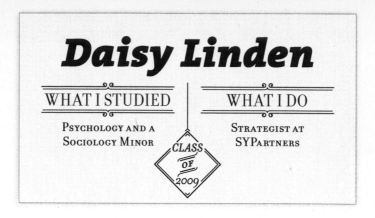

Daisy Linden

WHAT I STUDIED	WHAT I DO
PSYCHOLOGY AND A SOCIOLOGY MINOR	STRATEGIST AT SYPARTNERS

CLASS OF 2009

"I lived at home for seventeen months after I graduated."

Compared to her college friends, Daisy tried really hard to get a job senior year. That meant interviewing with almost every recruiter that came to campus, going to several job fairs, and sending out numerous résumés and cover letters. "What I didn't realize through this stab-in-the-dark search was I had no idea what I wanted to do," she said. "More than that, I didn't know *how* to figure out what I wanted to do." While packing her belongings after graduation, Daisy was anxious but not sad. "I was *not* ready to move out. But I loved home, and was lucky enough to drive there with my dad and brother, which was really cathartic, and distracting enough that I didn't get too sad about leaving."

As a freshman, Daisy had wanted to go into marketing or advertising, despite not understanding how they differ. By senior year, her plans had changed, and she wanted to go into consulting.

"The summer after senior year, I spent a month at a business school in a program designed for young non-business majors to learn about the business world. Through the Stanford Institute for General Management (SIGM) at the Stanford Graduate School of Business, I learned about strategy and finally got some meaty marketing classes, and most revelatory, learned about innovation as a business discipline. It gave me a great sense (missing from my liberal arts curriculum) of what parts of business school I'd like and which I wouldn't, and which disciplines (strategy) were so fascinating that I knew I'd want to pursue them as a career."

Senior Year Regrets:

"I feel pretty happy about my search post-graduation. It all became clear and much, much easier once I knew what I was looking for, e.g., kind of company, kind of job. Searching without parameters is super frustrating."

What College Taught Me:

"Most of all, I learned that despite the red tape, you can't assume you won't be able to do what you want just because it's not immediately offered up. I think, and God, this is trite, that it really is all about passion. If you're lucky enough to know what you love, do not hide it. Connect with faculty who share your interests. What professor wouldn't be refreshed by a student who was really into their subject material? In terms of friendships, don't stress about having too few initially; social circles build organically. As for life lessons, study what you want, and don't worry about what comes next. So few people end up following a professional path set by their undergraduate academics. Love history, but want to be a chef? Really into psychology, but want to be in sales? Go for it."

Life in the Real World:

"Take a deep breath. Be patient. Keep in touch with your college friends. Learn how to cook if you can't already. Make friends with your parents. Buy some interview-appropriate outfits. Explore. Figure out what you want. Then go get it."

Advice for Graduates:

"Do research on what you want to do first. A simple litmus test is writing a cover letter. Does it feel like work? Like you're cringing at the words you're using? Probably not a good company for you. If it's something you're genuinely enthused about, it'll be easy to write that letter, and it *totally* shows when recruiters (or anyone else) look at your résumé. Proofreading and writing well in general can make the difference between the trashcan and a once-over by the right set of eyes that can get you in the door. It's easy. Just do it. *Always* have questions prepared for interviewers."

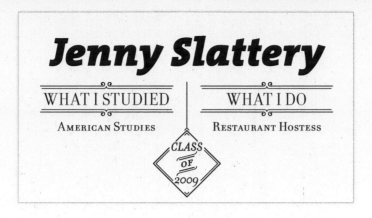

Jenny Slattery

WHAT I STUDIED
AMERICAN STUDIES

WHAT I DO
RESTAURANT HOSTESS

CLASS OF 2009

"I miss being in college and having all the time in the world to read, relax, and just hang out."

Although she best describes her thoughts during senior year as "a whole lot of figure it out later," Jenny did think about becoming a novelist or English professor. As a freshman, she was sure she was going to double major in theater and government. However, after taking a class in each subject, she realized neither discipline was for her. She went on to declare a major in American Studies, a department that involves writing, history, and literature. She graduated jobless, but sure of her desire to live in New York, so she slept on the couch in her grandmother's apartment in Manhattan while she searched for a job and began a new life.

Soon after arriving in New York, Jenny landed a job as a hostess at a restaurant in the East Village, but it didn't feel right. "That first year after college, I felt scattered, insecure, overworked, understimulated, and fairly unhappy," she explained. "Then, I saved up enough money to take two and a half months off. I used that time to clear my head, read, spend time with friends, visit home, and get a better sense of what I wanted."

Upon her return, as her desire for a career in writing and English blossomed, she decided she wanted to apply to graduate school.

"While a part of me feels not serious enough working in restaurants—I definitely have a complex about that at this point—I think I'm happier having a social job and moving around while I'm at work. Working at a job with varying hours also gives me good morning and afternoon time to write, read, and explore New York. A fixed 9-to-5 schedule sounds constrictive to me."

Senior Year Regrets:

"That's a tough question. In a way, I wish I had been more efficient and assiduous about looking for a job. On the other hand, I don't think I would feel as committed to pursuing writing and applying to grad school if I hadn't given myself space or worked in restaurants during this past year."

What College Taught Me:

"I learned so much in college. I had a great experience in classes, and felt my thinking was sharpened immensely. I learned the most, however, from the friends I made and the people I knew [in college]."

Life in the Real Word:

"In a way, being in the 'real world' is a crushing experience. But it's also very liberating. It's forcing me to look for the kind of life I truly want and to give myself the time to slowly discover and build that life for myself. There were many months when I was scraping together change from around my room, selling books and old clothes for money, debating with myself about whether

I could afford a bagel at Dunkin' Donuts, trying to live on ten dollars a day, or waking up on a couch to the sounds of my grandmother arguing with a stove repairman. All that has made living in my own apartment and earning a bigger weekly paycheck feel very luxurious, although it's much too easy to get used to spending money once you have it."

Advice for Graduates:

"Trust your instincts. Go for what sounds interesting, pursue a lifestyle that feels like it's leading somewhere, but also don't resign yourself to a career path just because it's a career path. It's important to be realistic, but it's equally important to find something you're passionate about, not just something that's 'responsible' or 'sustainable.' I see a lot of people I know who are committing themselves to jobs for two or three years because it seems like the adult thing to do, and subsequently feeling drained, unhappy, and just as lost as the rest of us."

Sebastian Junger

WHAT I STUDIED

ANTHROPOLOGY

CLASS OF 1984

WHAT I DO

AUTHOR (*The Perfect Storm: A True Story of Men Against the Sea*), DOCUMENTARY FILMMAKER

"The interviews mainly consisted of climbing a tree and going to work. It would be pretty clear if you could do the job or not."

As a member of the varsity track and cross-country teams, Sebastian was very focused on sports in his senior year, while all of his intellectual energy was devoted to his thesis on Navajo long distance runners. As a result, little thought was given to his future; however, the amount of work, time, and satisfaction in completing his thesis would wind up serving as a steppingstone to his journalism career.

Because he rarely, if at all, thought about his future, Sebastian was neither worried nor anxious when he graduated. The first job he got after college was with a construction company in Bedford, Massachusetts, near his hometown of Belmont. He was in good shape, so he was hired almost immediately. He continued to add to the "general labor" section of his résumé by working for a tree removal company that same summer. After a summer at home, he decided to move to Washington, D.C., and see what a new city could do for him. Like many other grads, he got his first job in a restaurant. As he thought about what kind of career and life he wanted, he recalled his pleasure in and excitement for writing his thesis.

"I wrote a thesis on Navajo long distance runners and just enjoyed it so much that eventually it occurred to me that that's what I wanted to do: research and write about things." He then began to write for a free weekly newspaper in Washington called *The City Paper*, and from there it became clear to him that he wanted to become an author. "I did not have any idea I wanted to be a writer in college...It just took a long time to get there."

Senior Year Regrets:

"I wanted to get my hands dirty for a few years, so I don't think I would have done anything differently. I might have traveled more."

What College Taught Me:

"I learned that the only things you're going to be good at are the things that arouse such passion in you that you'd risk your life for them. That is true of job, friends, politics, everything."

Life in the Real World:

"I've never managed to do it except at the most basic level of manual work, restaurants, etc."

Advice for Graduates:

"I would say don't sign anything until you've done a year of physical work and then used the money to travel around the world. If a desk job interests you at that point, then it's probably a solid choice."

Tyler Lohman

WHAT I STUDIED

GEOGRAPHY, GERMAN

WHAT I DO

PARTNER AND GENERAL MANAGER OF DOS TOROS TAQUERIA

CLASS OF 2008.5

"After I graduated, I did manual labor in a foreign country."

As a 2008.5 graduate, Tyler began and ended his college career in February. "By the time I was in my last semester, the majority of my friends had graduated the spring before, so that led me to be super-focused on school." With the heavy partying out of his system and only a few months to figure out life after college, Tyler turned his attention to WWOOF, the World Wide Opportunities on Organic Farms organization, which connects volunteers with organic farms and facilitates employment opportunities (on the farm) as well as room and board.

"I didn't apply to that many jobs while in college, but I did want to have *something* planned for those first few months after the summer. I always appreciate what has happened in my life and everything in the past, but I try to look at what comes next and not dwell too much." After only one interview, conducted over the phone while wearing only his boxers, Tyler was offered a position on a small farm in Italy where "I got to learn Italian and literally breathed in shit every day. Literally."

Tyler's time in Italy came and went quickly, as his job was only for three months. After coming home and moving back in with his parents, he gave himself a few months to relax and enjoy being a college graduate before he put out word that he was looking for work. "I had informational interviews aplenty, but nothing materialized. I did some volunteer work to stay active, however." A parent of a student who was in Tyler's mom's preschool class owned a small sustainable architecture firm and offered Tyler a position. "He gave me a job and could only afford to pay me $500 a month, but who was I to argue?" Between picking up crates of kale and asparagus and trying to determine the correct ratio of silt to hay, Tyler was in dire need of a change. "Most of my friends were living on their own, and I felt like the only one who was living at home. I had overdosed on farmer's markets and NPR, and it was time for a change."

Tyler decided to give New York a try, so he reached out to former high school classmates Oliver and Leo Kremer, the principal owners of Dos Toros Taqueria, about working for them. "I sat down and had a legit interview with them as they were opening their first restaurant, and I told them while in Italy I had washed cow intestines and was often covered in feces, so I could handle a lot when it comes to food."

According to Tyler, both brothers found his statement somewhat comical, but since it was true, they also appreciated it. Initially hired as an independent contractor, he helped develop the menu, ordered supplies and machinery, and secured permits. Often working six days a week, he was eventually promoted from independent contractor to partner and general manager.

Senior Year Regrets:

"In preparation for senior year, I wish I had done more summer internships. I should have utilized my time better by volunteering or doing something I could put on the résumé. I should have explored an interest I had. I was too caught up in trying to make money during summers, since I never really had any, so I waited tables. I wish I had used my off time better."

What College Taught Me:

"Personal relationships are the most important thing. I look back, and every step of the way, the reason I have gotten where I am now is because of personal relationships. I wouldn't have come to New York City if I didn't have a housing connection. I wouldn't be an owner of a restaurant if I didn't have a personal relationship. Take advantage of networking. Don't be afraid to ask for help."

Life in the Real World:

"I had some experience before leaving on my own in Germany (where I studied abroad), so I kind of knew what to expect. It's something that doesn't happen just like that. You learn over time how to live and adapt. You learn different things at different times. You learn to pay bills and then you learn to live with people. It doesn't happen all at once."

Advice for Graduates:

"You have to find what is most important to you. For me, when I came out of school it was being close to friends, geographically speaking. It wasn't as big of a deal to come to New York City, since I had a network of friends from school and home. What matters most to me are relationships and a landscape. I didn't go to a place for a job. A lot of people tend to apply for a job based on a cool company or how much the salary is, and you can end up wherever. In my own mind, if you go into a job strictly because it seems cool or makes a lot of money, where you don't know anyone, it's not a good call. Find your priorities and determine what relationships mean the most to you. Keep your ears and eyes open all the time. Look for connections."

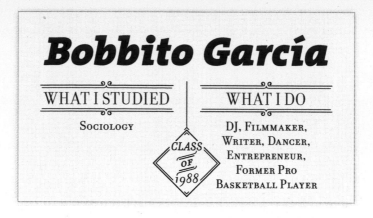

Bobbito García

WHAT I STUDIED	WHAT I DO
Sociology	DJ, Filmmaker, Writer, Dancer, Entrepreneur, Former Pro Basketball Player

CLASS OF 1988

"I never needed the validation of teachers, coaches, or corporate America to show who I really am and what I'm capable of."

Bobbito was on academic probation twice in college, first as a freshman and also during his senior year. "Education wasn't my thing," he said. "I was one of seven Latinos in a class of six hundred plus, and although I didn't know what was going to come next, I was psyched to be graduating." Following graduation, he moved home to New York and contemplated his next move. He took a job working for his cousin in a shop that sold animal and human skeletons for photography purposes. As a lover of basketball and music and a person with great social skills, he was looking into various industries, which led him to DefJam Records. "I got hired at DefJam as a messenger after I told Russell Simmons I would work for free. I was one of the first twelve people there."

Bobbito was determined to move up with the then small company, and decided he would work harder than anyone else. He was quickly promoted, and his always expanding and incredibly diverse career began. "For me, college taught me how to learn.

But I had examples back home of people in New York who had done well for themselves that didn't go to college, so I was able to use my experience in both worlds to help me become who I am."

Q&A

Senior Year Regrets:
"Nothing, really. I'm not ashamed or anything of how things played out, and I ended up in a good place."

What College Taught Me:
"I learned that if you have the work ethic, passion, and drive, nobody can deny your happiness."

Life in the Real World:
"I struggled harder in college than when I graduated. College was fuckin' hard, yo! I graduated in [the] bottom ten percent of my class. Twenty years later, *The New York Times* is reviewing a book I wrote [*Where'd You Get Those? New York City's Sneaker Culture: 1960-1987*]. There hasn't been one person that asked to see my grades. I got cut from varsity basketball three years in a row in school. During spring break junior year, I was playing basketball in New York and got scouted to play professionally in Puerto Rico. It showed me that I can create opportunities for myself outside of the college set if I work hard."

Advice for Graduates:
"No matter what work environment you choose or where you end up, survey the entire range of what can be done and figure out what's missing. Figure out what hasn't been done yet and think about what you can possibly do or corral help to make it happen.

Also, pay off those student loans before you buy a car, a house, jewelry, and all that."

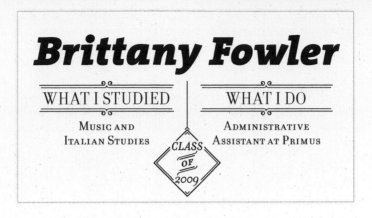

Brittany Fowler

WHAT I STUDIED | WHAT I DO

MUSIC AND
ITALIAN STUDIES | ADMINISTRATIVE
ASSISTANT AT PRIMUS

CLASS
OF
2009

"I went to Italy after college for a few months, but I did not want to move there permanently because I realized my specific career and life goals could not be fulfilled living there"

When Brittany started college, she saw herself going to graduate school or being the recipient of a Fulbright or Rhodes scholarship after college. Therefore, during her senior year, she did not actively look for jobs, but instead applied to graduate schools for vocal performance and various scholarships. She was accepted to only one school and, unfortunately, the acceptance did not include any financial aid. She thought about working full time in Italy, where she had studied abroad during her junior year, but jobs were very hard to come by and teaching English in Europe was not a realistic option, given her financial situation. "From what I could gather," she said, "teaching English would at best net 600 euro per month, which wouldn't be enough to cover my student loans and other bills, much less rent, especially in a large urban center."

Throughout the process of contemplating her post-college plans, she was upset that the college chapter of her life was ending, but also ready for the next one. "I was sad school was ending, but at the same time, I wanted to go out and finally live independently."

After moving home to Maryland following graduation, Brittany began applying to jobs in New York that specialized in foreign languages, thinking that was her best option to secure employment. She came up empty, so she then turned her attention to temp agencies in Washington, D.C., and was hired at the Theodore Roosevelt Conservation Partnership (TRCP), a non-profit corporation that works to preserve the traditions of hunting and fishing. Simultaneously, Brittany decided to continue to explore her personal contacts in search of a job she would enjoy more and called her uncle, a physical therapist, to see if he could help with possible opportunities in New York. "One of my uncle's clients worked at a hedge fund and said they needed an administrative assistant," she said. "I sent a résumé and cover letter, had three different interviews, and a week later was offered the job."

Following her first full week with the TRCP, Brittany quit. "Because it was the job I wanted more (plus it was in New York, with better pay), I chose Primus [the hedge fund] over TRCP. I was worried what TRCP would think of me leaving for resigning so early, but when I discussed my competing offer with TRCP, they said they understood because one, I was still in the 'temporary' phase with them, and two, they could not match the salary."

Senior Year Regrets:
"I would have been more aggressive with networking."

What College Taught Me:

"Accountability, privilege, social justice, and Italian."

Life in the Real World:

"You schmooze, you network, you make crucial connections that connect you to other people who in turn open doors for you that otherwise might have remained closed. Even in a field like opera, where musical talent is critical, the singers who get furthest along are the ones who know how to network and make the most of the connections they meet by staying in touch throughout the years. I got the interview for my job with Primus through a connection; had I just applied to them via Monster or some other career site, I wouldn't have been surprised if my résumé had ended up in the trash just like many others. I can actually do something about my dreams and aspirations instead of fidgeting impatiently at school, waiting until I graduated and was finally in a position to take more independent action. And if I want to go out and have an espresso at a nice café, I can actually go and do it without getting crap from my parents!

"When they ask, 'Are you a good fit for our 'corporate culture?,' they really mean, 'Can you conform with little to no struggle?' Corporate America is not that funny. There are no Dwight Shrutes [character from NBC's *The Office*] to inadvertently brighten your day."

Advice for Graduates:

"Start networking early. Tap into friends and families. Government jobs should definitely be considered, since they're merit-based, secure, and they pay reasonably well. Go forth! Accept unexpected opportunities that don't follow your plans. Try new things. Don't go to grad school right away. Struggle a little."

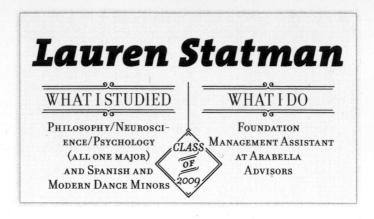

Lauren Statman

WHAT I STUDIED

PHILOSOPHY/NEUROSCI-
ENCE/PSYCHOLOGY
(ALL ONE MAJOR)
AND SPANISH AND
MODERN DANCE MINORS

CLASS OF 2009

WHAT I DO

FOUNDATION
MANAGEMENT ASSISTANT
AT ARABELLA
ADVISORS

"It was definitely important to me to focus on spending quality time with the people I loved on campus."

Lauren's freshman year centered on figuring out what college was like, meeting new people, and getting involved in student activities. That sentiment carried her through her senior year, when she focused on looking for ways to establish a post-college life, join a community in a new city, and strengthen her professional skills. "In general, I knew that I would find something great to do," she said. "It wasn't worth devoting all of my free time to that job search when I could be enjoying my last few months on campus."

While she worked to update her résumé, Lauren reached out to a few contacts to have informal conversations about her job search while also working on various program applications. The organizations and programs were all in the social/non-profit sector, with varying missions such as consulting, Jewish community organizing, and philanthropy.

To prepare for the in-person and phone interviews, she made sure to focus on three key aspects. The first was to browse through the website of whatever organization or company in which she was interested. Next, she would read over the description of the position she was applying for and map out how her skills and experience met everything they were looking for, while also compiling a list of questions to complement the job description. Lastly, for her phone interviews, like a singer before a performance, she exercised her voice for several minutes before speaking, and made sure to stand up and be as expressive and professional as she would in person.

In March of her senior year, she was accepted to the Washington, D.C., branch of AVODAH, a Jewish organization that fights against the causes and effects of poverty in the United States and champions social change. "I was really excited for the next step," she said. "I was just so relieved to actually have a plan! And a plan that I was excited about!"

Senior Year Regrets:

"I'm still happy with the way I went about it. I wasn't in a rush! I just knew something good [would] work out."

What College Taught Me:

"I learned that it really pays off to take the time to sit down with people and ask about their professional journeys, graduate programs, and important life-shaping experiences. They can tell you about interesting fields you didn't even know existed! [They can also] help you identify some 'next-steps' to help enter into those fields."

Life in the Real World:

"Happy hour prices are *awesome* and you should go to alumni events in your city!"

Advice for Graduates:

"First of all, don't underestimate how helpful one last summer after college can be. It can be a great time to establish yourself in a new city, stay at home and enjoy a summer there one last time, or have adventures all over the world! Also, whenever you apply for a job anywhere, reach out to your professional contacts—from internships or student activities—and your relatives to see if they have connections at the place you're applying to. You never know! And those connections can help you get your foot in the door and get an interview; beyond that, it's up to your merits!"

Sidney Kohls

WHAT I STUDIED | WHAT I DO

Art History, Visual Culture Studies | AmeriCorps, Friends of Children of Walla Walla

CLASS OF 2010

"You will get a job. You are hirable. And soon you will be able to afford drinks besides malt liquor."

After spring break, Sidney had a change of heart and was happy school was coming to an end. "Socially, there was nothing appealing," she said. "I already had my friends—I didn't want to go out to parties and pretend I wanted to meet stupid freshmen. I was also pretty burnt out on school." However, as soon as graduation came and went, anxiety began to overwhelm her. With no concrete plan, the only thing she was sure of was that she did not, by any means, want to live with her parents. With few alternatives, she thought it would be a good idea to move back to her college town and work with a volunteer organization, since she was familiar with the area and had access to current and former students through the alumni network. "I ended up doing AmeriCorps for a non-profit called Friends of Children of Walla Walla, which is like a Big Brother/Big Sister program. The job involves administrative duties, volunteer recruiting, and special event planning."

Senior Year Regrets:

"I am still glad I didn't spend my last months in school preparing for the real world. I really felt bad for the people who were too concerned with tomorrow to consider what they were missing out on at the time. That said, I wish I had more of a *mental* plan. I wish I knew I was going to actually apply for AmeriCorps more than a few weeks before I finished my application—I think that really would have eased my mind."

What College Taught Me:

"I learned not to take anything for granted. Higher education is a privilege, as is everything that goes along with it. I learned a lot about relationships and what is and is not healthy in all types of them. I learned how to balance school, sports, friendships, partying, [and] romance, and for that I am very grateful. I feel way more grounded, flexible, and mature than I was as a freshman."

Life in the Real World:

"You have to be persistent. You have to do things that make you uncomfortable. You have to put in the time to get the results."

Advice for Graduates:

"Travel after graduation. It's the only time you'll have for a while, probably. Figure out how to write your résumé and cover letters early. I wasted precious job-searching time because I was busy working on that stuff and refining it over and over. If you know for sure what you want to do, go for it. But if you don't, don't worry about it."

BAD INTERVIEW

"I was recently interviewed for a sales position at a winery. It was supposed to just be a conversation about when I would be able to come in for an interview, but ended up being a phone interview. It was 8:00 a.m. I was dazed and hungover. So, upon being asked why I wanted to work at that particular winery, I said, 'Well, I've tasted your wine, and it's *good*.' Needless to say, I did not get a second interview."

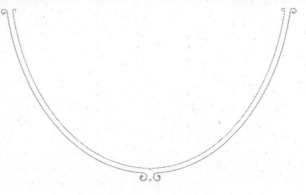

The Path-Switchers

THOSE WHO THOUGHT THEY
KNEW WHAT THEY WANTED TO DO,
BUT CHANGED THEIR MINDS.

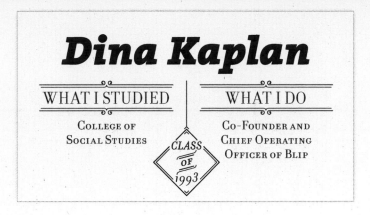

Dina Kaplan

WHAT I STUDIED | WHAT I DO

COLLEGE OF
SOCIAL STUDIES

CLASS
OF
1993

CO-FOUNDER AND
CHIEF OPERATING
OFFICER OF BLIP

"I definitely believe you can accomplish anything you set your mind to as long as you have no pride and a bit of chutzpah."

Unusual in that she took the fall semester off during senior year—to work for former President Bill Clinton's presidential campaign—Dina felt disenchanted when she returned for her final semester. "I had seen a taste of the other side, working with a group of people for a common goal," she said. "I knew that I would enjoy the working world, and I was really excited to get started on a career."

As a freshman, Dina found her career ambitions were "somewhere between a ballet dancer and a TV reporter." By her senior year, however, she decided that she wanted to work for MTV News.

"During my senior year, I had painstakingly gotten myself an internship at MTV News, but the week before graduation they told me I would have to sign a document saying I would be getting college credit for the internship. They were basically asking me to sign a false document. I told them I couldn't do it, and they said it was a deal breaker."

The day after she graduated, Dina called every single person she knew from the Clinton campaign to ask if they knew about any job openings at the White House. Her shot in the dark proved successful, as one of her contacts was looking for a Director of Research for The White House Counsel; they offered the position to her on the spot.

Senior Year Regrets:

"I would have asked earlier about what the requirements were for an internship at MTV News! If I had known I needed to forge a document, I could have prepared better for another job. But everything definitely worked out for the best, and I got there in a paid role a year and a half later."

What College Taught Me:

"I learned from college how important being a good writer is. When we're hiring at Blip, I can tell immediately—from an e-mail or a résumé—how smart someone is by how good of a writer they are."

Life in the Real World:

"Getting a job requires confidence and chutzpah. And relying on your connections. So stay in touch with people you believe in, and someday they may help you find a job. People also like to work with people they like, so being friendly and positive is a plus. Or become a computer programmer and you'll always be employed for life."

Advice for Graduates:

"Figure out what you want to do by speaking with a lot of different people, and then go for it. Don't let anything hold you back—anything and everything is possible."

MY FIRST
TV JOB

"I have a funny story about getting my first job as a TV reporter. I targeted the place I wanted to work and then called the Executive Producer of that newscast every single Friday for nine months. After all that time, however, he still didn't hire me. So one day I drove three and a half hours in the hopes that he would meet with me. He did! And I asked for one day of work on air. He gave it to me, and I was hired. It was a pure and simple case of persistence paying off."

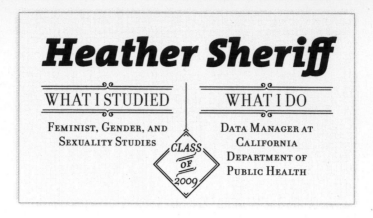

Heather Sheriff

WHAT I STUDIED

FEMINIST, GENDER, AND
SEXUALITY STUDIES

CLASS OF 2009

WHAT I DO

DATA MANAGER AT
CALIFORNIA
DEPARTMENT OF
PUBLIC HEALTH

"[After graduating,] I was pumped to finally have a space that was really mine and to get to make choices about where and how to live."

Heather toyed with medical school, public policy, and non-profit work during her senior year. She couldn't make up her mind and, ultimately, decided the best choice would be to find a job that allowed her to explore several options while making enough money to live on and save up. Mostly excited, but also a little anxious, she was ready to start something new following graduation. "Since I'd been working and supporting myself since high school, the idea of being on my own didn't seem terribly scary to me. I was pumped to finally have a space that was really mine and to get to make choices about where and how to live," she said.

As a freshman, Heather had been convinced she would be attending medical school once she finished college, but by her senior year, there were doubts. "I'd mostly discounted it because of my skepticism about the profession as a whole, its financial burden, and incongruity with my desired lifestyle, e.g., family, not working more than one hundred hours per week." After graduating, she moved to San Francisco. She had always wanted to live there, and it was near her hometown. Using Craigslist, she was hired as a personal assistant, but quit after four months once the "boss' crazy" got to her. She turned back to Craigslist, through which she was hired for a non-profit position as Data Manager for the California Encephalitis Project, which was run out of the California Department of Public Health. She now has thoughts about becoming a nurse-midwife and believes her current path will provide her with the experience and financial security to do so.

Senior Year Regrets:

"I probably would've stressed out about it a little less since things worked out pretty well for me."

What College Taught Me:

"College taught me how to really question the world around me, how to think critically about my world. I also learned a tremendous amount about myself—what I care about, what I'm good at, what I'm not—and about my relationships with other people. College showed me just how much more I have to learn!"

Life in the Real World:

"Personally, I really like the 'real world,' and I function really well as a self-sufficient person."

Advice for Graduates:

"Know thyself! And get interview and résumé/cover letter feedback from at least three different places. Also, apply to at least ten jobs a day if you're serious—it takes way more work than you probably think it does! Also, I'd say make good financial choices and take some time to enjoy yourself. It's really hard to make new friends post-college if you don't have a network in place, so don't underestimate the value in living somewhere near your friends."

Robert Block

WHAT I STUDIED

POLITICAL STUDIES AND
ECONOMICS

CLASS
OF
2009

WHAT I DO

TEACHER AND
FREELANCE WRITER

"Bringing girls home when you live at home is always a bit ridiculous. My suggestion is to sleep out."

Throughout high school, Robert had been fascinated with politics. His interest continued into college up until his junior year, when the idea of being a screenwriter took over. "Freshman year, I wanted to go into politics or something crazy. Since junior year, screenwriting has been the goal. While the dream of being a politician will never die, for now it is all about making movies," he said.

Through a family friend, Robert interviewed with Illumination Entertainment during his senior year for a researcher and reader position. Shortly after the interview, he was told he got the position, but after three weeks of waiting for information pertaining to his start date, salary, and responsibilities, he was told that the company couldn't afford to hire him due to the economy at the time. "There were a few other jobs I applied to that involved writing in entertainment and as a tutor that I was interested in, so I wasn't stressed too much."

Going to college in Los Angeles has its perks: great weather, proximity to the beach, and, if you are interested, Hollywood. For a hopeful screenwriter, it was more than ideal.

"I interviewed with Illumination, Blau and Associates, and William Morris Endeavor. I really enjoy the interview process and used Craigslist big-time. I didn't really prepare, just got a good night's sleep and did some background research on the company. It is always good to have some information walking in the door so that you can direct the conversation to areas you are strong in, as well as respond in ways that align with the company's beliefs."

Senior Year Regrets:
"I think I did all I could. When I was looking for a job, I would apply to several different jobs a day and really get after it. It's not college anymore, so you can't afford to waste any time in the job search."

What College Taught Me:
"Well first off, life is all about connections, so make sure to meet as many people as possible. Someone may not have a job or a hookup for you at some point in life, but you can definitely learn something from everyone. With that in mind, college is a great time to further hone yourself and improve yourself as a person, both academically and socially."

Life in the Real World:
"Getting a job just requires the determination to put in the work. There is always an opportunity to be had; if you want it, you can find it. Make sure to use all your resources: CareerBuilder,

Monster, Craigslist. If you are serious about finding a job, you need to stalk their pages."

Advice for Graduates:

"Start early and have something lined up, but if you hate it, quit. It's not worth forcing yourself into a career that you do not enjoy. Always push yourself to find a job that is right for you. If you aren't enjoying what you are doing, it is not worth your time, and you may end up trapping yourself. Hang in there and don't sweat the small stuff. School is amazing and the first few weeks—if not months— after graduation you may miss it a lot, but trust me, it gets better. The potential you have once living in the 'real world' is endless, and you are making significantly more money than you had in college, so there is still plenty of fun to be had. Just make sure to keep your head up, and do whatever makes you happy; these are the few years in life you can really just pick a direction and go for it. There is tons of time to settle for mediocrity down the road; shoot for the stars now."

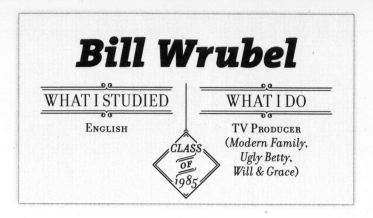

Bill Wrubel

WHAT I STUDIED	WHAT I DO
ENGLISH	TV PRODUCER
	(*Modern Family*,
	Ugly Betty,
	Will & Grace)

CLASS OF 1985

"When you're a senior on campus, you feel like you're the king of the world. When you're twenty-two and in New York, you start at the bottom. It's humbling."

Bill recalls his few career thoughts during his senior year of college as "wildly misguided," as he wanted to be an investment banker despite not possessing any knowledge of the field upon graduating. "I had a campus interview with a New York bank and was surprised when I didn't get called in for a second interview. I just didn't have any understanding of what my English major and interest in theater and writing might mean when it came to a job," he said. "I had zero connections in that world." He was certain he wanted to live in New York, but experienced a rude awakening when he had a tough time separating from the feelings and lifestyle of a student. "I really missed the easy access to friends and fun that was part of college life."

As a freshman, Bill had had an interest in politics and life in Washington, D.C., but it quickly disappeared after taking just one government class. He soon discovered that his passion lay in reading and writing, which led him to write his own play during senior year.

"So I ended my four years at college with the hope of becoming some kind of a writer, but I didn't quite know how to make that happen." Following graduation, Bill had several informational interviews with a variety of banks and advertising agencies, and also for sales positions, that didn't lead to anything. "I was ill prepared for them; I didn't have any idea what I wanted to do…I kept expecting that the person interviewing me would take some great interest in my future and figure out what I should do."

Through one of his friends, Bill interviewed for, and was accepted in, the page program at NBC, which serves as a primary pipeline to entry-level positions at NBCUniversal and a steppingstone for the world of entertainment. This program proved to be the starting point for Bill's career, as he continued to write and develop creative skills while meeting and working for those who worked in entertainment.

Senior Year Regrets:
"Honestly, I don't think I would have done anything differently. It's sad, but true. As aimless and naïve as I was, the experience of figuring it all out was important…I look back on college with great affection because I was so innocent and happy. Yes, I was in for a rude awakening. But I like to think I picked up some wisdom along the way as I was forced to grow up."

What College Taught Me:
"College taught me so much about creative thinking and the

importance of hard work when you care about something. I was a middling student until my senior year, and then I found myself in classes that I loved, and I put in the effort, and I was rewarded, not just with better grades, but with the thrill of learning. It sounds corny, but it's true. Senior year in particular, my own self, outside the world of my parents, finally started to emerge."

Life in the Real World:

"Know what you want. The people who succeed are the people who go after a specific goal. The only way someone can help you is if they understand what you need. So don't say, 'I want to be a writer or maybe a director of documentaries or perhaps a reality TV producer.' You need to say, 'I want to write for a show like *The Sopranos*.' Or, 'I want to be a producer of a show like *American Idol*.'" Then people can give you specific, clear advice. You will do so much better by having a specific goal that you can articulate. Hey, that goal might change, and that's fine. But you either need to be focused or act like you're focused. And then save your self-doubt for your friends or your shrink."

Advice for Graduates:

"Do what you can to understand what you like to do. Ask yourself, what are the things you've enjoyed studying? What are the things you have a talent for? I didn't know what kind of writer I wanted to be...I certainly never imagined writing for television. But writing was one thing that teachers had encouraged me to do. Paying attention to the things that you've enjoyed. But the bottom line is, you just don't know. It's trial and error. Live your life. Enjoy your early twenties. Some of the happiest people I know didn't figure things out until they were older."

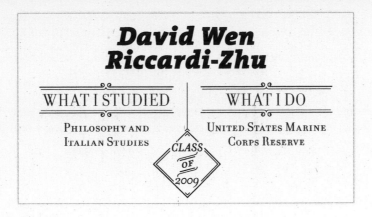

David Wen Riccardi-Zhu

WHAT I STUDIED
PHILOSOPHY AND
ITALIAN STUDIES

CLASS OF 2009

WHAT I DO
UNITED STATES MARINE
CORPS RESERVE

"I switched to the [Marine Corps] Reserve after pressure from parents two months after signing an active-duty contract. As soon as that happened, I realized I was unprepared for alternatives."

David prides himself on being a "jack of all trades more than a specialist" while maintaining that he has never had a dream job in mind. For as long as he can remember, he possessed a profound passion for the United States Marine Corps and becoming a Marine. He was so eager to begin his journey into the Marines that he did not walk with his fellow classmates on graduation day, instead receiving his diploma the week before so he could enlist as early as possible. "I wanted to go active right after high school. I delayed it by four years mostly because my parents really put the pressure [on me] to go to college first. I think they hoped I'd give up the idea during those four years. Instead, by the time I graduated, I was chomping at the bit," he said.

What David didn't realize, however, was that he was enlisting not just himself in the military, but his entire family as well. He began to see and experience the stress and anxiety that comes with serving in the Marines, and sought to find some middle ground where both he and his parents could be satisfied. Therefore, he voluntarily switched to the Reserves and turned his attention to other professions that could be safer and potentially provide more stability, such as photography and law.

"I would like a job where I could feel all of my different faculties and capacities engaged. Unfortunately, the world doesn't need men like me anymore. [I would like] something challenging that requires all my abilities put into use." He decided the best route was to obtain a law degree, so he is studying for the LSAT, as he believes the degree is very versatile and can be used in several different capacities. He is, however, ready and able if he ever gets the call.

Senior Year Regrets:

"I should have done research and networked. I wish I [had] prepared more and gone to seminars. I wish I had a résumé done and all options fully researched."

What College Taught Me:

"Academics were more or less disappointing. I had only a few outstanding professors in comparison to high school, where I had only a few not-outstanding professors. The few college professors that I thought were outstanding were really outstanding. I learned mostly life lessons and achieved personal growth due to being in an environment that I disliked and even resented. Spending a year abroad was great for personal relationships, and the extracurricular activities helped me mature."

Life in the Real World:

"The real world is a lot better than college. As for getting a job, only that having immigrant parents (who are also very solitary and thus don't have many American friends) makes the whole process of graduate education and finding work something totally new. I feel like a trailblazer. My father found work at the United Nations when he was twenty-three; he was placed there by the Chinese government and has worked there ever since. My mother came here with a medical degree—a career path chosen at nineteen—and with substantial work experience from Italy. It's been tough to get a sense of direction even in simply trying to find an approach to the matter."

Advice for Graduates:

"Definitely consider the military. It's an extremely fulfilling experience. It might set you back compared to your peers, but the lessons learned are life-worthy. Explore your options. I highly, enthusiastically, recommend the military experience. I would not, in fact, be against making it compulsory. People at college talked about diversity. The Marine Corps was a thousand times more diverse. It will open your mind more than your average ganga-addicted college hipster (who thinks he's more talented than us dumb grunts) might like to admit."

Randy Cohen

WHAT I STUDIED	WHAT I DO
Music	WRITER, HUMORIST, RADIO SHOW HOST, FORMER ETHICIST COLUMNIST FOR *The New York Times Magazine*

CLASS OF 1971

"One of the jobs I had in New York was emptying ashtrays at The Electric Circus on St. Marks Place."

Randy was rejected by every college he applied to with one exception. "For whatever reason, Vanderbilt wanted me and before I got there, I was looking forward to it. But in the end it turned out to be a disaster," he said.

During his freshman year, he was under the impression he was going to be surrounded by tons of interesting people doing interesting things, but was rather disappointed and frustrated. "I was at some big, dumb frat school in Nashville, Tennessee. Honestly, though, if I had been more sophisticated and open I could have made something of that experience, but I didn't. I really made a mess of my undergrad education."

Randy dropped out of Vanderbilt following his freshman year, but continued to live in Nashville after he joined a rock band, something he had been interested in since high school. Shortly thereafter, he moved to Philadelphia to play in a different band and enrolled at Pennsylvania State University. "Some of the guys in the band went there, so I went there, but only for two quarters. Then I dropped out again."

With his interest in music steadfast, Randy was out of school for six months while he tried to perfect his musical range and talent before enrolling at the State University of New York at Albany. Deciding to take himself and his classes very seriously, Randy declared a music major, the idea being he would go to graduate school to continue studying composition. "I got a full ride to California Institute of the Arts, where in exchange for free tuition, I had to teach two undergrad classes the basics of using a synthesizer, which wasn't a bad deal."

In his last year of his M.F.A. program, Randy was overcome suddenly with a life-changing thought: he had no musical gifts whatsoever. He decided that he shouldn't give up, so he finished his schooling and graduated. He moved from Los Angeles to New York City, where his band Jack Ruby was formed.

"CBS actually put us in the studio, cultivating our dreams of glory," he said. "We were all so excited thinking our moment had come. But like all bands, we went nowhere. CBS decided not to sign us and then we were on our own. To support myself I needed a day job and began working for Steve Rutt, who designed the first video synthesizer."

At the suggestion of a former bandmate, Randy officially gave up on music and gave stand-up comedy a try. After a few gigs and performances in various clubs in New York, he realized that even the best comedians had day jobs and decided to pursue other options. He started to write and submitted various works to newspapers that usually had a comedic or humorous tone. "At first it's a flat-out rejection, then a personalized rejection, then a handwritten rejection, then a rejection with some edits, [and] then they accept you."

As his credentials and skills expanded, so did his opportunities. His work began to appear in *The New Yorker*, *Harper's*, and *The Atlantic*, which led to book deals with publishers. Additionally, he worked as a writer for 950 episodes on the *Late Show with David Letterman*, sharing three Emmy Awards for Outstanding Writing. Arguably, his biggest addition to the show was the creation of the "Top Ten List." Perhaps his most significant work came as a writer for *The New York Times*; he authored *The Ethicist* column from 1999 to 2011, in which he answered questions from readers on a weekly basis.

Senior Year Regrets:

"I would have actually gotten an education! I was meant to get a liberal education, but it didn't work out that way because of my interest in music. I should have been an English major. I was very ill-educated. I was composing some of the ugliest music you have ever heard. I was not good at music but kept going with it."

What College Taught Me:

"Most important thing I learned was in my second year of my M.F.A. program. I learned I had no musical ability of any kind. Ideas form themselves in their heads and it comes to you, but I had verbal ideas about sounds. I didn't think *in* sounds. The ability to think musically does not guarantee you will have interesting music. But if you can't think musically, if you don't think in terms of sound, you are absolutely in the wrong field. I had no musical gifts of any kind. Part of that was due to lack of self-knowledge. How many contemporary composers do you follow?"

Life in the Real World:

"The important thing about all this is how long it took me to figure out what it was I wanted to do. You don't know what you will be good at. You won't know what you have the temperament to do. College lets you try things just because you are interested in them. You learn about endeavors and you learn about yourself. I made a mess with my education, so it took me longer than the normal person. I was searching around for business and work. I didn't know what to do with myself. I thought to myself, 'What can I do that is verbal, funny, and I can make a living?' I thought I could write for the newspaper and that led to everything else."

Advice for Graduates:

"Finding something you like doing that you actually might be able to do and pursue with a full heart. Forty years later, after I graduated, things aren't perfect. There are patches where I get nice work, sure. Other times the world isn't welcoming, but all in all, this suits me. The lesson is if you are a doofus like me, it may take you longer to figure out what you wanna do."

MY FIRST "APARTMENT"

"In my first year of grad school I lived out of a van. I parked my van in the driveway of a friend and ran an extension cord from his house to my van, where I had an electric blanket. I had some kitchen privileges and could use his bathroom, but my van was my home."

Jim Shepherd

WHAT I STUDIED	WHAT I DO
GOVERNMENT	ANALYST AT MITCHELL MADISON GROUP

CLASS OF 2007

"Be nice to everyone you meet."

As a government major, Jim believed his degree would be very useful. He hoped to go to law school after graduating, something he had planned on since his freshman year. However, after interviewing with various consulting firms on his college campus and in New York City, Jim switched his plans from law school and government work to the life on Wall Street. The simple fact that the recruiters were on campus and going after students resulted in something more tangible and immediate compared to that of applying to law school and hoping for something to materialize.

"The consulting firms and investment banks just lined up on campus. I got kind of lured into it, despite the fact that it probably wasn't for me," he said. "Coming from a liberal arts background, I felt like I underwent tremendous intellectual growth over the course of my four years in college, but I didn't exactly have a specific path etched out like some of my friends who went to other kinds of schools, which was empowering, but also frightening in a way."

Prior to all of his interviews, Jim spoke with his college career office and contacted alumni who worked at any of the companies he was interviewing with. He never once used Craigslist, but found out about all of his opportunities through the career center and alumni networking.

Senior Year Regrets:

"I would have taken advantage of internship and job-shadowing opportunities throughout college so I could experience potential career paths before having to make a decision senior year, to find out what I liked, and what I didn't like, so I knew what I was getting into upon graduation. At the time, I was very excited to graduate, but now that I am in the working world I miss college life and wish I had appreciated it more."

What College Taught Me:

"That the relationships you build can be lifelong and the experiences you have can never be replicated."

Life in the Real World:

"Don't settle for a career path that you aren't passionate about. Changing it up and starting something new isn't the same as quitting. That's what the years immediately after college are for: figuring out what you love."

Advice for Graduates:

"Nothing is more important than networking. The more people you know, the luckier you get."

Peter Schube

WHAT I STUDIED

HISTORY AND ENGLISH

WHAT I DO

PRESIDENT AND CHIEF
OPERATING OFFICER OF
THE JIM HENSON
COMPANY

CLASS OF 1981

"I actually enjoyed my college experience more in retrospect than at the time."

Following an enjoyable and successful college career during which he made a number of significant and lasting relationships, Peter was ready to get to work. In December of his senior year, he was offered a position as a paralegal at a law firm in New York City that was an ideal setup for him. "We had a family friend who was a partner there at the time," he said. "It was all lined up. I wasn't stressed." Believing college was keener on developing the individual rather than building a community, Peter welcomed the idea of living and working in New York while meeting and interacting with different people on a variety of levels. However, there was one major drawback.

"I had to live at home. My mom begged me to live at home and I didn't want to, but I really didn't have a choice. There is nothing more emasculating than a twenty-two-year-old man living at home with his mother." He spent a year as a paralegal before quitting and leading a program for high schoolers in Greece that he had participated in when he was in high school. The time abroad was something he probably wouldn't ever be able to duplicate; it gave him the time to think about what he wanted to do with his life. After he returned to New York, he realized that law school was his best option and applied to New York University, where he was later accepted.

Senior Year Regrets:

"Nothing. I couldn't have asked for an easier transition. It was great to work one year, go abroad for a bit, and come back."

What College Taught Me:

"Most of what you learn is what you figure out in hindsight. College, at the time, is a little too raw and intense while you are doing it. You are a stupid young person. There are so many teachable moments and learning opportunities in college that you don't realize until you have already graduated. I discovered at my twenty-fifth reunion that the connections I made were stronger and more powerful than I realized."

Life in the Real World:

"It's always hard. College was a lot easier."

Advice for Graduates:

"A lot of people want to get into entertainment. No general qualifications. Meet everyone you can. Be as relentless as you can and chase down all opportunities. Get into it! It is much easier to get a job in the business you want to be in once you already have a foot in the door."

Ken Magarie

WHAT I STUDIED	WHAT I DO
MATHEMATICS AND ECONOMICS	HIGH SCHOOL MATH TEACHER, VOLLEYBALL AND SOCCER COACH

CLASS OF 2009

"Don't chase down the perfect job if it is unrealistic. Either look for something that you have previous experience in, or follow those sweet parental hookups."

While many recent graduates are moving to new cities and wondering how much of their income will go toward their housing costs, Ken is living rent free at a private boarding school in Illinois, where he teaches math and coaches volleyball and soccer. Graduating from college with over $20,000 in student loans, Ken was willing to take any job he was offered. Fortunately for him, a position as a geometry and algebra teacher became available, and from there the coaching positions were later offered. He is eating for free (in the dining hall), living in a one-bedroom apartment with complimentary cable and Internet, and is involved in two areas he loves: teaching and sports.

While in college, Ken was convinced that he would not have a problem finding a job. "I thought to myself, 'My sweet math-econ degree from my sweet well-respected college will get me a sweet finance job, and I'll make bank.'" Once senior year came around, he began to think otherwise. "My lack of experience in anything besides tutoring and camp counseling, combined with the fact that I did not do great in any econ classes, will make it extremely hard to get the finance/business job that I always assumed I'd just get." Instead of getting down on himself about not doing very well in his classes and having little to no experience, he decided to pursue a career where he could use his tutoring and camp background: private preparatory schools.

Ken's very first interview was during his senior year with a middle school close to campus. Because of his experience and confidence, he did little to prepare and assumed he would have a relatively easy time with the interview. Unfortunately, the interviews did not go according to plan. "I thought I knew what I was doing, but I didn't have a lot of questions to ask," he explained. "The other girl who was there interviewing for an English teaching job asked a lot of good ones." He then applied to boarding school positions and made sure to change his approach to the interviews.

"For my interview [at my current job], I met with a bunch of people and then taught a class. If I have just as much teaching experience (none) as someone, I will have the upper hand if I can coach multiple sports, was an R.A. in college, etc. Boarding schools are often looking for people who are 'triple-threats,' [who] can teach, coach, and work in the dorms."

Senior Year Regrets
"Not much. It worked out pretty well."

What College Taught Me:

"In college, I learned that you have to live life to the fullest, as cliché as that may sound. I can't stand having regrets and I feel like I left [college] with very few."

Life in the Real World:

"In the 'real world,' I've learned that money makes the world go 'round."

Advice for Graduates:

"Don't chase down the perfect job if it is unrealistic. Either look for something that you have previous experience in, or follow those sweet parental hookups."

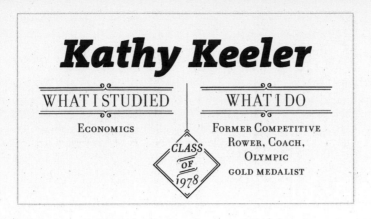

Kathy Keeler

WHAT I STUDIED	WHAT I DO
ECONOMICS	FORMER COMPETITIVE ROWER, COACH, OLYMPIC GOLD MEDALIST

CLASS OF 1978

"I was not ready to move on."

Before she began her freshman year, Kathy had a vague notion that she wanted to be an architect. Plans changed, however, as she developed an interest in becoming a doctor and began taking pre-med courses.

"I was thinking that pre-med or chemistry might be the thing. Placing into organic chemistry freshman year and struggling mightily, the reality of eight more years of school got me off that track by sophomore year. I looked at many other majors and finally picked [economics] because I really liked the professors that I had gotten to know. I passed chemistry, but it was very touch and go for a while there," she said. "I was done after my freshman year with pre-med." She decided it was best to take classes from professors she liked, believing that it might result in a genuine interest in the subject.

Although her interests in academics varied, she found stability and joy as a member of the women's crew team. By the time senior year came around, she was preparing for what she believed to be her last year rowing competitively. "My roommate senior year applied to a bunch of jobs and got a bunch of rejection letters. But still I wasn't too worried about finding a job. I figured something would work out," she said. Following spring break, Kathy's coach told her that she had been invited to try out for Nationals and, due to the intense training schedule, subsequently missed Senior Week and all of the festivities, events, and parties that came with it. She did, however, return for graduation day to receive her diploma and walk with her classmates.

The tryout lasted a few months, and at the end of the summer, Kathy was cut before the final roster was set, which resulted in a move back home with her parents. Without many leads for job opportunities, she arranged a meeting with the principal of her high school and was offered the position of junior-varsity basketball coach.

"I applied for some economic research jobs, but I had always been a jock and had an interest in sports. I did have some idea of going to grad school, however, but that never happened."

Once the school year ended, she moved to Vermont for the fall with a friend to work at a bed and breakfast before moving to Florida during the winter. She then tried out for Nationals for a second time; unfortunately, she was the very last woman cut from the team. All was not lost, however, as she knew the head women's rowing coach at the University of Pennsylvania, who helped her get a position coaching the school's freshman women's team.

In 1981, after a year of coaching, Kathy decided to take a year off from all things rowing; she moved to Boston and worked for a consulting firm. "I remember sitting in that office and looking out the window and thinking, 'I should be out there.'" After one year with the firm, she quit and decided to give rowing one more shot. She applied for and accepted the women's crew head coach position at Smith College, where she also trained for one last shot at the Women's National Team. She made the team in 1983 and won gold in the Women's Eights at the 1984 Olympics in Los Angeles.

Senior Year Regrets:

"Nothing, really. The whole job process while in college isn't worth stressing over [during] your senior year."

What College Taught Me:

"I learned that you can actually get to know your professors. You can talk to them or anyone, really. You don't have to feel put off by who they are, [or] what their title is."

Life in the Real World:

"The real world for me was about rowing, so it wasn't that much different than in college. The whole job thing was secondary."

Advice for Graduates:

"What have you always wanted to do? When you graduate college it is time to do something you have always thought about. Do something outside the box. Right after you graduate is when you don't have any outside things that tie you down. You can go to Africa. Don't follow the route and get a financial job in New York."

Photo by Maren Ellingboe

Ari King was born in 1987 in Oakland, California. In 2009, he graduated from Wesleyan University with a B.A. in Italian Studies. He believes everyone has a story to tell regardless of age, education, background, or career ambition, and that everyone can benefit from the advice, suggestions, and experience of others. He currently resides in Brooklyn, New York, but will always call California home. This is his first book.